Prana Vidya

With kind regards, ॐ and prem

Swami Niranjan

Prana Vidya

From the teachings of

Swami Satyananda Saraswati
Swami Niranjanananda Saraswati

Yoga Publications Trust, Munger, Bihar, India

Prana Vidya

From the teachings of Swami Satyananda Saraswati & Swami Niranjananada Saraswati

First published as *Prana Vidya* 1976 by Bihar School of Yoga.
New edition published as part of *Prana Pranayama Prana Vidya* 1994 by Bihar School of Yoga

Published by Yoga Publications Trust
First edition 2013

ISBN: 978-93-81620-78-6

Publisher and distributor: Yoga Publications Trust, Ganga Darshan, Munger, Bihar, India.

Website: www.biharyoga.net
www.sannyasapeeth.net
www.satyamyogaprasad.net

Printed at Thomson Press (India) Limited, New Delhi, 110001

Dedication

In humility we offer this dedication to
Swami Sivananda Saraswati, who initiated
Swami Satyananda Saraswati into the secrets of yoga.

Dedication

To our guru Sri Swami Satyananda Saraswati
who continues to inspire and guide us
on our yogic and spiritual journey.

Contents

Preface

Prana vidya, literally 'the science of the life force', has been a part of every spiritual tradition since time immemorial. The basic principle underlying every aspirant's effort is accessing the energy latent in the individual and in the cosmos. Terminologies have differed, methods have varied, but transformation has come about only when the vital force has been channelled, whether directly or indirectly. In the Indian tradition, the seers used a particular term to denote the knowledge of this process: prana vidya.

References to prana vidya can be found in the Upanishads, dating back to 500 BC, and in later works such as *Yoga Vasishtha*. The pertinent verses seem to indicate that the principle of prana vidya was widely employed by seekers since the vedic times. However, there is no specific guidance provided in the texts; it was always left to a master to interpret the notion according to his individual experience and pass the knowledge down to a deserving disciple. In addition, unlike pranayama which has a more or less standard methodology, the scope of prana vidya is much wider. Therefore, different masters used different paths by which an aspirant could unfold and direct the latent energy. The tantric tradition, for instance, evolved its own system of awakening energy using the scheme of *chakras*, energy plexuses, and *nadis*, energy channels.

In the 20th century, Swami Satyananda Saraswati, a *siddha guru*, perfected master, distilled the essence of several esoteric practices from the ancient texts and guided aspirants in their application. Through the depth of his own yogic understanding, he gave the practices a structured form which allowed one to systematically deepen the experience. These included yoga nidra, pranayama, ajapa japa, antar mouna, pawanmuktasana, shankhaprakshalana, as well as prana vidya.

Swami Satyananda's approach to prana vidya was based on tantra. He used the science of chakras, nadis and mantras to identify and influence the energy patterns in the body. This would, on one level, bring about greater vitality, healing, as well as shifts in mental patterns. Gradually, the aspirant would experience prana as pure light connecting him or her to the source of life and consciousness. In the final stage, the practice would become the pathway for merging with *mahaprana*, the cosmic energy.

The original teachings of prana vidya by Swami Satyananda were captured in the text *Prana Vidya,* published in 1976. Over fifteen years later, in 1994, Swami Niranjanananda Saraswati published the text *Prana Pranayama Prana Vidya,* which expanded the initial teachings. Over the years that followed, a new vision emerged and it was decided to present the teachings in two volumes: 1. *Prana and Pranayama*, and 2. *Prana Vidya*.

Prana and Pranayama was published in 2009 and offers essential understanding of the principles of prana, both yogic and scientific, and includes a stage-by-stage description of the practices of pranayama as taught in the Satyananda Yoga tradition by the Bihar School of Yoga. This text, *Prana Vidya,* constitutes the sequel and explores a wider dimension of prana.

The division of the volumes indicates that an aspirant must first acquire an understanding of prana and develop proficiency in pranayama (under the guidance of an experienced teacher) before moving on to the more advanced practice of prana vidya. Therefore, prior to attempting the practices outlined in this text, one should make a thorough reading of *Prana and Pranayama* and try to perfect the practices given therein. Even so, whether one is ready to commence prana vidya sadhana can only be ascertained by a master.

The content of *Prana Vidya* is divided into two parts. Part One discusses the theory of prana vidya, exploring it as a meditation technique, a tool for acquiring the knowledge of prana, an art and science of healing, a skill to influence and control prana at will, and more. It also includes research conducted by leading scientists worldwide – supporting the notions of yogis and healers whose timeless wisdom has inspired people for centuries.

Part Two covers the practices. Chapters 7–10 detail various practices to prepare and maintain the body, mind and pranas for prana vidya. Chapters 11–16 outline the stages of prana vidya in a systematic way. Two of the final chapters include practices that relate to healing oneself and others through the conscious channelling of prana. The last chapter provides two class transcripts of advanced prana vidya with Swami Satyananda and Swami Niranjanananda, respectively.

The first stage of prana vidya commences with practices designed to awaken prana. The next stage involves practices that raise and store the awakened prana. The more advanced practices facilitate the expansion and distribution of prana internally, throughout the body, and externally, into the surrounding environment. Each progressive stage aims to develop and further refine pranic awareness, sensitivity and control. It is imperative that each stage is mastered before moving on to the next; this may take one month, one year or more. There should never be any rush to move on.

As the practices unfold, many psychic experiences manifest and guidance often becomes necessary. Thus, success in prana vidya requires regular practice and patience, and adherence to the master's instructions. If one stays firmly on the path, one will eventually experience *dhyana*, complete absorption, and *samadhi*, union with the self.

Theory

1

Prana Vidya: An Introduction

There are two basic principles of the universe: *prana shakti* and *chitta shakti*, energy and consciousness. They are separate entities existing in duality, yet they are the opposite poles of the same principle. Thus, changes in the state of consciousness can be brought about by changes in the level of prana and vice versa. (See *Prana and Pranayama*, pp. 2–4, 9–19.)

Tantra works on the principle that expansion of consciousness is specifically brought about by the liberation of energy. Therefore, even if one 'meditates' for one thousand years, if there is no liberation of energy then evolution of consciousness is not possible. Although modern psychology cannot explain this process, the science of tantra has always known that the awakening of prana or the liberation of energy is the key to superconscious states. The question then arises, how is this latent energy released from within the fold of matter? The shakti which lies within the body is a fantastic force, but how can it be manifested? It is well known that scientists have released nuclear energy from gross matter. How can prana shakti be released from the body? This is the aim of tantra and prana vidya.

Science of prana vidya

At the level of the individual, *prana* is the vital energy flowing within the body to keep every organ alive and active. This individual life force is a part of universal prana, just as individual consciousness is a part of universal consciousness. *Vidya* means meditation or knowledge. Thus, *prana vidya* means knowledge of the life force, meditation on the life force, or realization of the life force – first at the individual level and eventually at the cosmic level.

Prana powers the body and mind in the same way that electricity powers machinery. The *Yoga Vasishtha* says (3:17):

बहुनाऽत्र किमुक्तेन सर्वमेव शरीरके ।
करोति भगवांवायुर्यंत्रेहामिव यांत्रिकः ॥

The divine vital air, prana, does quite everything in the body, as a machinist performs the activities of a machine.

Just as the voltage of electricity can be increased, the store of prana in the body can be increased. A low voltage of electricity will run small machines, light bulbs and heaters, and so on. That same electricity, however, when circulated many times through armature, winding or rotating coils, can create an enormous amount of energy. It can generate electricity of 10,000 volts and have the capacity to power big generators and illumine whole cities. This same electricity can, under certain conditions, be converted into the most powerful laser beams. The power and capacity found in laser beams is nothing other than a higher state of ordinary electricity.

In prana vidya, a similar method is used. Using intense concentration, one-pointed awareness and visualization, psychic energy is circulated through specific pranic channels in the body. After some time, this generates vast amounts of prana shakti. In fact, prana vidya progressively develops awareness and control over the field of prana to such an extent that it brings about an awakening of that great potential which lies dormant within the depths of one's being. It is said in *Yoga Yajnavalkya* (7:20–21):

स्थानेष्वेतेषु मनसा वायुमारोप्य धारयेत् ॥
स्थानात्स्थानात्समाकृष्य प्रत्याहारं प्रकुर्वतः ।
सर्वे रोगा विनश्यंति योगाः सिद्ध्यंति तस्य वै ॥

> One must focus and retain the prana, with the help of the mind, in vital points. For one who does pratyahara, drawing the prana from one point to another, all diseases are destroyed. For him yoga attains fruition.

In this text, prana vidya is presented in a systematic way that allows the practice to gradually unfold. Each chapter covers an essential stage of prana vidya that includes a range of relevant practices. The practices have been chosen to facilitate an experience and understanding of each aspect of prana vidya. It must be remembered, however, that the selection of practices within this text represents merely a taste of the vast scope of prana vidya.

The pranic body

According to yoga, a human being is capable of experiencing five dimensions of existence, which are called *pancha kosha* or five sheaths. These are: i) *annamaya kosha*, the physical body ii) *pranamaya kosha*, the pranic body iii) *manomaya kosha*, the mental body iv) *vijnanamaya kosha*, the psychic body, and v) *anandamaya kosha*, the bliss body.

In prana vidya, one is concerned with the pranic body, which consists of *chakras*, energy plexuses, and *nadis*, energy channels. There are six chakras: mooladhara, at the perineum (men), cervix (women); swadhisthana, at the coccyx; manipura, at the navel; anahata, at the heart; vishuddhi, at the throat; and ajna, behind the eyebrow centre. There are two other energy centres which are often grouped with chakras: bindu, at the top back of the head; and sahasrara, at the crown of the head.

Nadis number at 72,000 or more. Out of these, there are three major ones that are frequently utilized in tantric practices. These three nadis run within the framework of the spinal column and are named ida, pingala and sushumna. *Sushumna nadi* is the central energy channel and is associated with spiritual energy. Ida nadi and pingala nadi spiral around sushumna in opposite directions, converging

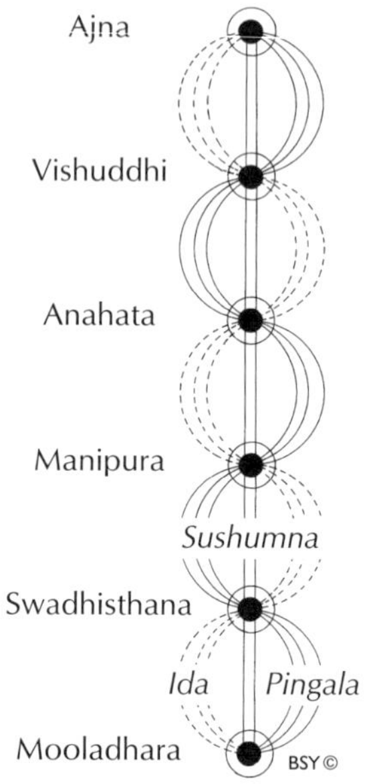

at each chakra from mooladhara to ajna. They represent the dual forces of mental energy and vital physical energy. At ajna, the nadis converge and flow together up to sahasrara. (See *Prana and Pranayama* pp. 20–59)

There are various techniques that facilitate and expand one's experience of the pranic body. Initially, subtle sensations such as heat or tingling indicate the presence of prana in different parts or regions of the physical or pranic body. As one becomes more proficient in prana vidya, pranic awareness becomes more and more refined until the pranic flow is experienced as currents of energy and visualized as particles of light flowing through the nadis. When perception becomes completely attuned to the pranic body, a body of light may be seen in which there are thousands of delicate, wire-like structures conducting *shakti* or energy. These are the nadis. There are thousands upon thousands of nadis within the substructure of the gross body and they distribute consciousness and prana to every atom. *Yoga Vasishtha* describes the subtle nature of the nadis that constitute the luminous pranic body as (3:19):

सहस्त्रविनिकृत्ताङ्गाद्बिसतंतुलवादपि ।
दुर्लक्ष्या विद्यमानााऽपि गतिः सूक्ष्मतराऽनयोः ॥

The channels of vital energy are more difficult to perceive than a section of a lotus-fibre whose body has been cut into a thousand, and existing therein, the movement of these (pranic fields) is still subtler.

At times these rays of light are actually seen, at other times there is only a memory of this light. The discovery of these passages of light in memory, in dreams, in thought, in visions, or in imagination is the discovery of prana.

Basis of practices

Prana vidya is an exceptionally subtle, yet powerful practice that requires patience, intense concentration and refined perception. It begins with techniques that awaken prana lying dormant within the pranic body. The generating station for prana is mooladhara; the storage centre is manipura and the distribution centre is ajna. Generally, prana vidya practices awaken prana from mooladhara chakra. After awakening and raising prana from mooladhara, it is taken to ajna chakra which becomes the temporary storehouse and distribution centre for prana. Once sufficient energy has been generated and stored in ajna, it is distributed to different parts of the body. Prana can also be extended further afield and directed externally to transform the environment and to heal and uplift others. Before concluding the practice, it is important to return the awakened energy back to mooladhara, the original source.

When prana is raised from mooladhara, it is directed along a pranic pathway. There is sometimes confusion regarding which pathway to use and the do's and don'ts of this stage. In prana vidya, pingala nadi is the main nadi used for raising prana, as it represents the more extroverting vital energy within the pranic body. Circulating prana through pingala awakens and expands this solar energy. Therefore, one should aim to become proficient in the techniques incorporating pingala nadi. One may also use sushumna, either as a preliminary technique or as an advanced technique, depending on how the teacher guides one. However, a beginner should not use ida nadi to raise prana, as it is the pranic channel for the introverting flow of mental and lunar energies. If ida is utilized prematurely there is a risk that the mental forces will become dominant and could subjugate the pranic vitality. This potentially could lead to physical and mental instability. When prana is returned to mooladhara at the end of the practice, generally the sushumna passage is used; ida or pingala are used only in specific instances.

There must be a correct understanding of the three flows of ida, pingala and sushumna before commencing the practices of prana vidya. Finally, do remember that the spectrum of prana vidya is wide and a master's guidance is necessary to determine how one should proceed.

Pranayama to prana vidya

Pranayama acts as a stepping stone that leads one naturally to the practice of prana vidya. The numerous pranayama techniques available develop awareness and control of the breath, which indirectly awakens and expands prana. During pranayama, a certain amount of creative force is generated throughout the entire body, influencing the existing quantum of prana. In the *Yoga Sutras* of Sage Patanjali, pranayama is said to activate the psychic centres and to create a condition in the brain by which the inherent psychic faculties are released. As a result, the mind becomes fit for concentration.

With regular practice, pranayama cultivates a deeper, longer breath and the ability to retain the breath effortlessly. This quality of breath is necessary for prana vidya, as the breath and prana move as one force slowly up and down the psychic and pranic pathways. Breath retention is required at the end of the inhalation while storing prana at ajna. The flow of breath and breath retention need to become effortless so the awareness can be focused exclusively on prana.

Ujjayi pranayama is a tranquillizing pranayama used throughout prana vidya. Tranquillizing pranayamas pacify the body and mind while simultaneously increasing the pranic capacity and conscious control of the mind, body and pranic interactions. Ujjayi pranayama is known as the psychic breath since it leads to very subtle states of mind and psychic sensitivity. It is an indispensable aspect of prana vidya and may be practised from any position: standing, sitting, or prone. When the ujjayi breath is used in meditation, it is performed through both nostrils with natural inhalation and exhalation, and *kumbhaka*, retention, is omitted. (See *Prana and Pranayama* pp. 60–61, 251–256.)

Initially, the breath can be employed as a medium to experience prana, to experience the vital life force flowing through each and every part of the body. By systematically moving the awareness and the breath through the different parts of the body, the mind gradually becomes sensitized to the flow of energy. The moment this occurs, breath awareness is transformed and pranic awareness commences.

Mapping the body

To fully understand and direct the flow of prana, it is necessary to have a thorough knowledge of the inner functioning of the body. Prana can be directed along a particular path (for example, the alimentary canal) if one has a detailed knowledge of the particular path. The prana may then be directed through the power of imagination. To give another example, prana can be circulated through any of the bones of the body if the practitioner has a detailed knowledge of the inner body structure.

This detailed knowledge of the body is essential for a successful practice of prana vidya. For instance, if one were asked right at this moment to touch the kidneys mentally, one would probably find it very difficult. Therefore, before beginning the practice of prana vidya, the kidneys, bladder, bones, blood vessels and other relevant parts of the body should be located, visualized and then touched by the mind with full awareness. Prana vidya can still be practised without this thorough knowledge; however, the practice will not be as successful.

In this context, yoga nidra is a helpful preparation for the practice of prana vidya. In fact, one may do a specific yoga nidra to develop awareness of different internal organs (see Chapter 9).

Benefits

Prana vidya practices gradually expand the quantum of prana within the individual. Such expansion occurs both internally and externally. The expansion of individual pranic awareness and capacity is reflected externally through greater levels of influence. In addition, energy blocks are released as prana is moved up and down the nadis. As energy is liberated, it becomes available for distribution, and the organs, muscles, bones, cells and atoms are nourished. More life-giving energy and less tension means the related systems of the body function more efficiently, effectively and harmoniously.

Negative states of mind and emotional tensions are overcome when prana flows freely and in abundance. The psychological state is reflective of the underlying pranic condition, and thus by directing the flow of prana, the mind becomes tranquil and calm. When the mind is steady and still, the ability to concentrate develops and the meditative states of dharana and dhyana are experienced.

Through prana vidya a deeper understanding and higher level of consciousness emerges in relation to prana and life. Prana can be utilized directly for healing oneself or others with the proper knowledge and understanding. With supreme mastery of prana, such as that possessed by a guru or spiritual master, prana can be directed into an object or place for worship through the practice of *prana pratishtha* (see Chapter 5).

Swami Satyananda said that the full benefits of prana vidya are experienced once complete mastery has been gained over the flow of prana. When this occurs, the entire body-mind is completely revitalized to such an extent that there is a sense of being reborn. Swami Satyananda uses the analogy of a musical instrument, such as a harmonium or piano. If two notes are played that are not in tune, it will create a slightly discordant sound. If more notes are out of tune, it will create a horrible cacophony. Prana vidya tunes the whole body so it can play a beautiful melody, the wonderful and joyful song of life.

2

Meditation and Prana Vidya

The mind is connected to a huge reservoir of power; however, this storehouse of prana is generally blocked by anxieties, complexes and memories of past experiences. They use up much of its energy and the power of the mind becomes dissipated. Furthermore, modern life presents many distractions, which also affect the harmony of prana in the personality. As a result, prana shakti is generally in an agitated state. This underlying pranic condition is reflected in the physical and mental states. When the pranas are disturbed it is natural that thoughts, emotions and relationships will also be affected.

The eight-limbed path prescribed in Sage Patanjali's *Yoga Sutras,* outlines the way to pacify these agitations so that meditation becomes possible. The first four stages, the external limbs, are to calm the restlessness of the body, mind and pranas. Once the body and mind have been purified, the final four stages or the inner limbs, related to the progressive levels of meditation, reveal the more subtle layers of the mind.

The practice of meditation is a continuous process that releases mental tensions and unlocks blocked energy. The process is such that the more one purifies the mind, the nearer one approaches meditation; the more one is able to achieve and maintain the meditative state, the more one is able to remove the deeper, ingrained complexes. As one is able to remove the deeper, ingrained complexes from the mind, more energy becomes available. The result is a stronger, more relaxed and focused mind with an increased capacity to delve into the subconscious and unconscious.

Stages of meditation

The main path of Sage Patanjali's raja yoga is contained within eight stages: *yama*, social codes; *niyama*, personal codes; *asana*, postures; *pranayama*, control or expansion of prana; *pratyahara*, sense withdrawal; *dharana*, concentration; *dhyana*, meditation; and *samadhi*, superconsciousness. The first four stages are known as the *bahiranga*, or external limbs. In these initial stages, an effort is made to harmonize the physical, mental and pranic bodies in order to reach a state of total steadiness and equanimity. The final four stages collectively are known as the progressive stages of meditation or the *antaranga*, inner limbs.

Meditation begins with *pratyahara*, which translates as 'to retreat' or 'to return to'. Pratyahara includes methods to induce a state of mind in which the awareness is withdrawn from the external world. One interacts with the external world through the sense of smell, taste, sight, touch and hearing. Using specific pratyahara practices, these senses are systematically withdrawn from external stimuli and turned inward. Initially, during the practice of pratyahara, the mind is easily distracted and is in an inert or dense state. However, through regular practice tensions are gradually released from the mind and prana begins to withdraw from external sensations. Over time the awareness and prana become internalized and the state of pratyahara is achieved.

In meditation, when the mind is successfully withdrawn from the external world of the senses, it leaves only three things remaining in the awareness: the meditator, the object of meditation and the act of meditating. This is the trinity in meditation. There is no fourth experience, no experience of distraction, no dissipation, no knowledge or experience of time and space. There are many pratyahara practices that endeavour to achieve this state: yoga nidra, prana nidra, antar mouna, trataka, nada yoga, japa and kirtan, to name a few. These practices train the mind to withdraw the senses from the external world and to become aware of the internal world. Prana nidra is a unique practice in relation to prana vidya in that it serves the dual purpose of bringing about pratyahara as well as sensitizing the practitioner to the experience of prana (see Chapter 10).

The state of pratyahara is a fundamental stage of meditation. When the state of pratyahara is experienced and there is a relative absence of sensorial awareness, the mind becomes focused and a deepening of mental awareness occurs. This leads to dharana. *Dharana* can be translated as concentration or one-pointed awareness and is explained in the *Yoga Sutras* as (3:1): *Deshabandhashchittasya dharana* – "Concentration is binding the mind to one place." This place can be a mental or physical place, object or focal point. When the mind is concentrated in this way, perception becomes acute.

There are many dharana practices and almost any object can be used as the basis for concentration. In prana vidya the focus of awareness is on prana, the vital life force within. The common aim of all dharana practices is to train the mind to focus on the chosen object so that after a particular period of time, the mind becomes one with that form. Such dharana practices are not superficial; they involve diving deep into the inner dimensions of the mind and consciousness. Sage Patanjali acknowledges in the *Yoga Sutras* that meditation on an object one likes is a sure way to make the mind steady, controlled and peaceful (1:39): *Yathabhimatadhyanadva* – "Or else by meditation as desired, the mind can be steadied." Thus the aspirant should choose an object which motivates or attracts.

Another element essential for developing concentration is regularity in practice and Sage Patanjali emphasizes the need for abhyasa. *Abhyasa* is constant, regular and uninterrupted practice with faith and conviction over a long period of time. During this period of regular practice, the mind alternates between steadiness and dissipation. As deeper tensions are dissolved, the mind and prana become more and more focused. Dharana is achieved when the pranas become concentrated and the awareness is directed toward the object of meditation without being disturbed by any mental patterns. Once the mind is able to hold the form for a length of time, the ego withdraws itself and the state of dhyana, sustained awareness, occurs.

Sage Patanjali describes dhyana as an uninterrupted flow of consciousness. The *Yoga Sutras* state (3:2): *Tatra pratyayaikatanata dhyanam* – "That uninterrupted stream of the content of consciousness is dhyana." *Dhyana* is concentration without a break. It literally means 'total, non-dual, absolute awareness'. It is an expanded and refined state of mind where the awareness deepens and you experience a state of deep, prolonged concentration. At this point, all the mental and pranic forces flow in one direction. Dhyana is a state of mind and consciousness in which there is alertness, dynamism, dissociation of the mind from the senses and total concentration. In this state, the internal world becomes vast and limitless to the extent that the external experience becomes part of the internal. As the internal experience of dhyana intensifies, simultaneously an appreciation of the purpose and beauty of life develops and deepens.

Beyond dhyana, once absolute awareness has been accomplished, the domain of samadhi is entered. When the trinity of experience: the meditator, the object of meditation and the act of meditating disintegrates, the boundaries are broken and at that time the seed of individual existence dissolves. That is the highest point, called samadhi, nirvana, emancipation. It has no name and it has every name. According to *Hatha Yoga Pradipika,* samadhi is a field of awareness that is superconsciousness. It is the result of a complete one-pointedness of mind and an expansion of consciousness from the mundane perception to that of cosmic awareness. It is the final experience of every human being and that which we are all evolving towards. Through yogic and tantric practices such as prana vidya, this process of evolution is accelerated.

Prana vidya

Prana vidya is a meditation practice on the vital life force within the body. It is a powerful practice, a complete sadhana in itself, and has the potential to take one from pratyahara to deep states of meditation. Prana vidya harmonizes the pranas, controls the vagaries of the mind, expands the pranic capacity, develops the ability to control prana and in so doing, directs the awareness into deeper spheres of one's own being.

Vidya is commonly translated as 'inner or spiritual knowledge, wisdom or science'. During the time of the Upanishads, vidya also referred to a practice of meditation or dhyana, for instance, the mantra vidya and atma vidya practices. The *Chhandogya Upanishad* describes the process or practice of meditation as ultimately leading one to the attainment of true wisdom, that is, to realize prana as the all-embracing cosmic life force. Thus, the word 'vidya' describes the process, the meditation technique and the wisdom gained, the knowledge of prana.

Each consecutive stage of prana vidya involves a subtler and more refined experience of prana. The practices commence with a process of awakening and raising prana. This process is repeated until it becomes effortless. Abhyasa is essential. It takes time and practice to train the mind, to release tensions and to harmonize the pranas. However, once the pranas are activated, the journey to the deeper mind, to the subtler layers, becomes clear.

In the next stages of prana vidya, techniques such as expansion, contraction, localization and visualization of prana are introduced. Prana vidya affects the mind indirectly through the awareness and manipulation of prana, as prana and consciousness are opposite poles of the same force. For instance, contraction of prana calms the turbulent tendencies of the mind. It concentrates the mind and stills the chatter. Expansion of prana stimulates and awakens the mind. During localization of prana, that is, when prana is directed to specific regions of the body, the mind is focused and strengthened.

Visualization of prana intensifies the effects of each practice and is a crucial aspect of prana vidya. Visualization is a technique that requires imagination, concentration and willpower to create a mental image and results in enhanced subtle perception. It is used to harness the power of prana, which is then controlled and directed by the strength of the mind for healing and other purposes. In the case of pranic healing, visualization of the body as well as the prana further enhances and amplifies the healing effects. Throughout the practices, prana is visualized as streams of light particles that flow within the nadis. At first, imagination is used; however, ultimately a vision of prana shakti as a luminous body of light is experienced and knowledge of prana awakens. According to Swami Satyananda, the art of visualization is best perfected through the practice of yoga nidra. (See *Yoga Nidra,* by Swami Satyananda Saraswati, Yoga Publications Trust, 2012, for a wide range of practices.)

Meditation on prana is a powerful practice, a complete sadhana in itself. Such concentrated awareness of prana not only purifies, expands and harmonizes the pranic body, but also awakens the psyche and eventually leads one to the experience of dhyana and beyond.

3

Disease and Pranic Healing

The physical body is a storehouse of pranic energy. Each fibre of the body is connected with prana by a complex system of *nadis*, or energy channels. The three major nadis are ida, pingala and sushumna. The six major *chakras* or energy vortices, are located where numerous nadis, including ida, pingala and sushumna, converge. Appendix D illustrates the location of the chakras. Each chakra governs and distributes energy to a specific region of the body. Energy is distributed to each and every organ and cell of the body through thousands and thousands of minor nadis emerging from the chakras. Thus, the functioning of the physical body is directly related to the quality and quantum of energy flowing within pranic body.

The pranic body and its matrix of nadis can be compared to an electrical system that distributes energy from the generating station to each house. Disease can be explained in terms of a faulty electrical system. In the case of insufficient voltage, lights become dim. In the case of a short circuit, the lights go out altogether. When there is an electrical failure, there is no light. The same applies to prana. Physical and mental vitality wanes when there are energy blocks, and where there is no prana, there is no life. Many colloquialisms use electricity as an analogy to describe disturbed pranic conditions, for instance, someone has 'blown a fuse', 'run out of batteries', 'burnt out' or 'lost their spark'.

The origin of disease

According to the ancient yogic texts, *annamaya kosha*, the physical body composed of *anna* or food, depends on prana for health and wellbeing. Gross forms of prana are needed in the form of food, water and air. Refined forms of energy are also required from the subtle bodies: *pranamaya kosha*, the energy body; *manomaya kosha*, the mental body; *vijnanamaya kosha*, the psychic body; and *anandamaya kosha*, the bliss body. The koshas are interrelated and the pranic body infuses prana directly into the physical body. Prana flows within and all around the body keeping every system, organ and cell of the body alive and active.

The prana that flows in the body has been divided into *pancha prana*, five energy fields in the body: prana, apana, samana, vyana and udana. They have been classified according to the location and function of the energy within the physical body. For example, *samana* flows sideways in the abdominal region between the navel and diaphragm. It governs and regulates the whole digestive system. (See *Prana and Pranayama,* pp. 48–59.)

The physical body works ceaselessly to maintain a state of balance or homeostasis, sustained and supported by prana. The body and mind are being continuously fed with stimuli from the external environment, whether from food, water, air, sound or interactions. In fact, anything and everything in life enjoyed through the sense organs: the eyes, ears, nose, tongue, skin and mind, is food for prana. Thus, maintaining the integrity of prana requires constant care and attention. When there is vitality in the pranic body, the whole body and mind remain vitalized and nourished and homeostasis is supported. On the other hand, when energy is depleted, the body and mind are affected and imbalance occurs.

Yoga Vasishtha (v. 712–720) explains that imbalanced prana leads to physical disease through improper digestion. If prana is blocked, depleted or excessive, digestion is adversely affected and nutrients cannot be properly absorbed and distributed. Pranic imbalance may also occur due to agitations in the mind, which also leads to digestive problems. When digestion is disturbed in this way, the physical body becomes weak and disease results. When prana flows optimally through the nadis it nourishes muscles, cells, organs and all other parts of the body.

Diseases that have their origin in the mind and manifest in the body are known as psychosomatic diseases. Diseases that arise first in the body and then travel to the mind are called somatopsychic diseases. Hatha yoga and tantra have described and prescribed techniques for dealing with both psychosomatic and somatopsychic illnesses. These sciences differentiate between the body and prana, the inherent life force within the body. This distinction indicates that the health and wellbeing of the body-mind is dependent on prana. In yoga, the hypothesis is that all diseases are ultimately caused by improper distribution of prana in the physical body. Even those diseases regarded as psychological in nature, are actually caused by an imbalance in pranic distribution.

Below are some examples of physical disorders resulting from a pranic imbalance in a chakra:

Vishuddhi chakra is a major distribution station. In the physical body, the chakra concentration point is situated at the junction of the neck and trunk. Vishuddhi distributes prana to the eyes, nose, throat, thyroid, parathyroid, thymus and other organs and glands in that area. If there is an improper distribution of prana to the thyroid, emotional symptoms occur. Many emotional complexes and problems are directly caused by hypo or hyperthyroidism, even when a disease condition is not clinically evident.

Manipura chakra is situated behind the navel in the spine. It is the main distribution centre for the digestive system and the adrenal glands that produce the hormone adrenaline. Improper distribution of prana from manipura chakra to the adrenal glands can result in fear psychosis, as well as somatic diseases such as colitis and hepatitis.

Swadhisthana chakra is located at the coccyx and is the distribution centre for the urogenital organs including the uterus, ovaries, urethra, kidneys and bladder. Improper distribution of prana to, or excess energy in, these particular organs can create frigidity or impotence. Though medical science might consider these to be purely psychological problems arising from childhood experiences, one has to remember the connection between prana and the body-mind. Childhood experiences may have agitated the flow of prana, which in turn has led to disturbed psychological states as well as physical disorders.

Pranic healing

> Just as the impurities of metals are burnt after being blown (by fire), similarly the abnormalities of the organs are removed by controlling prana.
>
> *Brihadyogi Yajnavalkya Smriti* (8:30)

The understanding of the nature of prana and the holistic approach in relation to healing the physical body can be found in many ancient civilizations. Traditional oriental medicine is one healing system that reflects a thorough understanding of the pranic body and its interconnectedness with the physical body.

Pranic healing, the science and art of healing with energy, is another such healing system. It has been used for millennia. Originally, pranic healing was only known and practised by the chosen few: the yogis, shamans, medicine men and traditional healers. The knowledge and art was transmitted directly from master to disciple, often involving a series of initiations or energy transmissions and for this reason, pranic healing has been shrouded in mystery. In recent times pranic healing has become more accessible, however. It is practised extensively by occult schools, spiritual groups and private healers throughout the world.

In the late 1970s, pranic healing was extensively researched in the countries of the USSR, Bulgaria and Yugoslavia. Much of this research has been documented in the book, *Psychic Discoveries Behind the Iron Curtain.*[1] Modern research is beginning to scientifically prove the effects of pranic healing and such studies have been outlined in Chapter 6. Pranic healing is also attracting a lot of attention from leading medical authorities, and investigations are underway to ascertain its uses in the modern medical setting. It is well known that in India, Tibet and China, pranic healers are an integral part of the medical profession. At the Apollo Gleneagles Hospital in Kolkata, India, for example, pranic healing is part of a holistic approach in the treatment of cancer. It is offered as a way of supplementing modern medicine and surgery as well as providing optimal psychological support crucial for health and wellbeing.

Elements of pranic healing

Pranic healing is called by many names: prana vidya, medical qigong, psychic healing, reiki, therapeutic touch, laying on of hands, magnetic healing, faith healing and charismatic healing, to name some of the more well known terms. Any form of true healing employs the same force and power notwithstanding the difference in method. The science of healing is based on certain natural laws of the body that must be observed to maintain health and can be utilized to restore health when it is lost. These natural laws include proper nutrition, elimination, breathing and more, all of which influence and are influenced by the subtle movement of prana in the pranic body. All healers are only channels of expression through which the natural forces and energies flow.

Each healing system has its own unique technique that has evolved from the culture and philosophy that surrounds it. For instance, in terms of yogic philosophy, the pranic body is detailed in terms of koshas, chakras and nadis. The practice of prana vidya, which facilitates the proper distribution of prana throughout the whole body, reflects this yogic philosophy.

Healers in the Philippines describe the pranic body in terms of auras.[2] They consider the pranic body, which surrounds the physical body, to be made up of two layers, an inner and outer aura. The inner aura is described as bioplasmic rays projecting perpendicularly from the physical body. Toxins, wastes, germs and diseased energy are said to be expelled by these rays, predominantly through the pores. If a person is weak from depleted energy, the rays droop and become partially entangled. The whole body becomes susceptible to infection because of the decreased capacity to expel toxins. The outer aura is recognized as being outside the inner force field. It acts as a container for the subtle energies and prevents pranic energy from leaking out. The healing techniques utilized to restore the body to health reflect this knowledge of the pranic body.

Pranic healers possess the ability to perceive prana at a subtle level and to manipulate prana for healing. Perception of prana and the directing of prana are crucial for diagnosis and treatment. At the core of pranic healing is the belief that health problems occur if prana is disturbed, that is, depleted, excessive or congested.

Pranic healers generally use their hands to scan the patient's body to sense the location of the pranic imbalance, which has resulted in illness, and to direct the subtle prana to facilitate healing. Irrespective of the technique utilized, the common remedy is to energize the deficient areas, cleanse the excessive areas and if needed, remove restrictive blockages.

To energize means to vitalize the body or a particular area with prana. Prana may be channelled from the universe as with reiki, from spirit as with spiritual healing, or prana may be awakened and channelled through such techniques as prana vidya. Symbols, visualization, pranayama and specific breathing practices, mudras and sound are examples of tools used by pranic healers to facilitate the flow and intensity of energy available for healing.

To cleanse means to purify and remove toxic energy. This can be done in any number of ways. Often pranic healers utilize a physical aid to facilitate the process. Fresh water, salt water, sand and smudging sticks made of sacred herbs are used to absorb toxic energy, to cleanse the aura or to purify a physical space. In some ancient traditions, diseased energy is sucked out through the mouth or removed with the use of twigs.

Once treatment is complete, physical exercises and breathing techniques are often recommended to support the healing process. Such practices supplement pranic healing as they expand the quantum of energy within the pranic body and help to maintain a balanced flow of prana within the body and mind.

Reiki

In 1822, Dr Mikao Usui, a Shingon Buddhist priest and physician, was guided on his own spiritual journey to search for the secret behind the miracle healings of Christ and Buddha. During his search, he rediscovered an ancient healing art detailed in an 1,100 year-old Buddhist manuscript, *The Tantra of the Lightning Flash that Heals the Body and Illumines the Mind*. From this ancient source, Dr Usui moulded a seven-level tantric teaching into what has become the modern-day healing technique known as reiki. The Japanese word *rei* means universal and *ki* is life force energy; together they describe the source of healing, the universal life force energy.

There are two essential aspects of reiki. The first is the simplicity of the technique. The healer, with sincerity and purity of intention, connects to and becomes a channel for the universal life force energy before commencing a healing session. The hands are then placed on the body of the person requiring healing. This is done in a specific sequence designed by Dr Usui. Vital energy flows from the universe through the healer to the person being healed. A principle of reiki is that the body uses its own innate wisdom to draw in what it needs for healing. Reiki increases and balances the vital energy of the body and mind. It also exposes them to a much higher vibratory frequency of energy, allowing energy blocks to be penetrated and dissolved. As such, there is no methodology in the system of reiki and energy is never sent wilfully. The reiki healer simply acts as a channel for the universal life force energy that facilitates the healing process. The second essential aspect of reiki is the use of attunements that open the channel to the universal life force energy. According to Dr Usui, they are closely connected to the energy transmissions or empowerments related to the Healing Buddha. Traditional reiki is taught through a direct lineage that goes back to Dr Usui and flows directly from the master to disciple. Once the disciple has perfected the art of reiki under the guidance of the master, the disciple may become empowered through additional attunements to initiate others. In the advanced stages of reiki, symbols are used to intensify the healing energy, for distance healing and in other reiki healing practices.

Therapeutic touch

In an experiment conducted in the US and overseen by Dr Krieger, professor of Nursing Education at New York University, sixty-four patients were divided into two groups. One group received the 'therapeutic touch', palm or psychic healing, from nurses twice a day. The control group received only routine nursing care. After the first day, the therapeutic touch patients began showing significant increases in the haemoglobin levels of their blood. No significant changes were found in the control group, the untreated patients.

The power of touch and words is captured in the *Atharva Veda* (4:13, 6–7):

अयं मे हस्तो भगवानयं मे भगवत्तरः ।
अयं मे विष्वभेषजोऽयं शिवाभिमर्शनः ॥

Felicitous is my left hand, yet more felicitous is my right one. This hand contains all the healing properties; its gentle touch brings peace and welfare.

हस्ताभ्यां दशशाखाभ्यां जिह्वा वाचः पुरोगवी ।
अनामयित्नुभ्यां हस्ताभ्यां ताभ्यां त्वाभि मृशामसि ॥

With our ten-fold fingered hands, with our tongue that precedes the voice; with these two healers of disease we stroke you with a gentle touch.

Malaysian pranic healing

The 'laying on of hands' is a simple and effective method of pranic healing. Different methods are employed in other cultures. Carol Laderman, an anthropologist, studied psychic healing in Malaysia, where a shaman employs music and chanting to induce trance states.[3] She originally tried to remain purely objective in her research; however, she eventually submitted herself to a twenty-minute trance healing. She describes it as follows: "As the music became louder, my mouth opened, trembling uncontrollably. I began to feel cold winds blowing in my chest, winds that increased in intensity as the music swelled and accelerated until it felt as if a hurricane was raging within my heart."

In the Malaysian tradition, which mirrors yogic understanding, mental processes, talents, desires, and so on, are classified as 'air' or 'inner winds'. When these are suppressed or not expressed, denied or thwarted, they become dangerous, causing 'wind sickness'. Shamans use their techniques to disperse those pent-up winds. Many techniques are available, from sensory deprivation to overstimulation, to produce altered states of consciousness. One of the most frequently used methods involves music, especially percussive music, with a steady four-beat rhythm. This rhythm is said to bring about an important transition, a state of trance, and is equivalent in its effect to theta brain waves found in deep meditation. This is the optimum frequency for pain relief and so is also utilized in the technique of electrically-stimulated acupuncture, another healing modality.

Transmission of energy

The transmission of prana is a natural event in our lives and it takes place all the time, whether we are conscious of the process or not. Vibrations or energy radiations are constantly being emitted from everybody, from everything. Some people have long, strong pranic radiations, while others have short, feeble radiations. Research with Kirlian photography has gone a long way towards verifying this hypothesis of pranic energy emission as a natural part of life.

Prana is potent, yet very subtle to grasp for the ordinary level of awareness. However, those people who are sensitive to energy can feel and see prana. Generally, they are born with this faculty and are natural pranic healers capable of healing the sick. They have not learned this science from a person or book. Often, they themselves are surprised at their own healing powers and may wonder where they have come from and how they work.

Few people are born healers, but most of us are capable of developing this ability to some degree through the practice of prana vidya. This technique not only opens up our awareness of the vast stores of energy within the human body, but also teaches us how to consciously use prana for the improvement of our own health and the health of others.

Vedic education

The *Atharva Veda* is the fourth vedic text containing tantric concepts. It is made up of a collection of mantras and describes the art of invoking divinity. It reveals the way towards this supreme state of consciousness through vedic education and spiritual initiation. It outlines two essential principles that underlie vedic education and mirrors the philosophical foundation of pranic healing. The first principle is that infinite energy, *prakriti* or *mahaprana*, pervades the universe. The second principle is that the physical world and physical body are the foundation for receiving this energy.

Vedic education describes three aspects of pranic awareness that support complete health and wellbeing: how to manifest cosmic energies in the body, how to increase the capacity to hold these energies, and how to expel from the body obstructions to the manifestation of these energies. By developing control over prana in this manner, one can remain connected with the divine and experience the joy of life.

References

[1] Ostrander & Schroeder, *Psychic Discoveries Behind the Iron Curtain,* Abacus, 1977.

[2] Master Choa Kok Sui, *Miracles through Pranic Healing,* Health Accessories for All (HAFA), Secunderabad, India, 1987.

[3] Laderman, Carol, 'Trances that Heal', *Science Digest*, July 1983.

4

Traditional Pranic Healing in India

In recent years, there has been a resurgence of interest in traditional healing practices as a means to cure and prevent physical and mental illness. Due to the increase in psychosomatic disorders and a search for more holistic systems of health, attention is returning to the ancient healing arts that have stood the test of time. India is no exception. In this land of diversity, ancient rituals permeate modern life and traditional healing remains prevalent in all strata of society. To many, these methods may seem to be superstition, and it is true that sometimes they percolate down in that form. However, at their core is an understanding of natural laws that lies beyond the range of intellectual reasoning, and their efficacy has been proven time and again.

Swami Satyananda has often related an incident from his youth when he watched a traditional healer at work. The incident stayed with him and over the course of time he understood the principle employed, which was a form of prana sadhana. In fact, this experience was the first trigger for his formulation of the system of prana vidya. The methods described in this chapter may be seen in this light.

Traditional pranic healing

As with many countries, a wide range of healing modalities can be found in India. The traditional healers are called *ojha*. They use their psychic and pranic abilities to diagnose and treat disease. They will often scan the body using their sensitivity to detect energetic disturbances that give rise to illness and disease. Once diagnosed, they manipulate the subtle energy to cleanse, activate and realign the pranic body.

The healing itself may be performed simply, using the hands to psychically feel and manipulate energy. Often healers also employ certain techniques or rituals to create an environment conducive for healing such as the use of incense, holy water, chanting, drumming, mantra, sacred symbols, slow breathing or rhythmical dancing. The energetically charged atmosphere allows the patient to enter an altered and receptive state which is crucial for healing to occur. During the healing sessions performed by the Bhopas in Rajasthan, for example, everyone joins in a circular two-step, hopping dance set to the rhythm of a drum. The drum beat and the steps in the dance create a kinaesthetic experience which facilitates a lulling of the conscious mind, rendering the unconscious mind more receptive to the positive imagery utilized by the healer.[1]

One distinctive characteristic of Indian culture is the role of the sacred and this is reflected in the healing arts. The sacred, in its myriad forms, is drawn upon to activate strong psychic energies inside and outside the patient. The rituals employed by healers are steeped in local custom and tradition. Some are even based on legends associated with the healer or healing centre. In many temples of the Mother Goddess in eastern Uttar Pradesh, those seeking healing are expected to offer fine red linen with a golden trim. To uphold local legends, patients are supposed to enter the Kali Temple in Chittor, Rajasthan, crawling. Due to the subtle nature of pranic healing, the patient may not know or understand the rituals or techniques being used. Despite this, for healing to take place, the patient needs to have complete trust and confidence in the healer and the healer's ability to heal. If there is no faith, pranic healers generally refuse to offer treatment. They know that without faith and trust, healing cannot take place.

Kusha grass method

Traditionally, when a baby has a fever, a *pandit* or priest is called to find out the nature of the illness; that is, to determine whether it is a physical, psychological or pranic illness. This occurs in villages, towns, rich and poor communities alike. If the disease is diagnosed as being more than simply physical, the baby is taken to a pranic healer.

In the healing process, from diagnosis to treatment, the local customs must be observed. One custom, for instance, is that the baby must be carried to the house of the healer by the parents themselves and never by an intermediary. Even the wealthy must undergo this ritual, therefore there is never any question of sending a car to pick up the healer. Some healers require the parents to bring a coconut for the healing, others require an erika nut, wrapped in a betel leaf and tied with a red thread. Once the customs have been satisfied, the baby is placed near the healer to diagnose and ascertain the location of the illness.

One well known technique involves the use of kusha grass. It is a special magnetic grass found in India, which is often used in spiritual and esoteric rituals. Through the medium of the kusha grass, the psychic healer uses his prana to feel the psychic illness in the child. The kusha grass is passed over the front of the body from the top of the head down to the feet. The process is repeated down the left and right sides of the baby until the kusha grass stops, apparently by itself, over the centre of illness. While moving the grass in this way, the healer is able to psychically see or feel the illness.

Evil eye

Though not acknowledged in many modern societies, the 'evil eye' is a commonly recognized cause of illness in many indigenous cultures. Just as we can transmit prana in order to heal, it is believed people can also send malevolent powers with the intention of hurting others. Ill-intent is transmitted, often through the eyes, causing unexplained fever, colds and other illnesses.

In order to diagnose the influence of the evil eye, the healer makes a concoction of burning charcoal, red chillies and mustard seeds in an iron vessel. It is placed near the patient. If the patient does not sneeze and cough, which is natural when smelling burning chillies, the problem is said to be the result of the evil eye. Healing is then performed to rectify this pranic disturbance.

Karmic illness

In some instances, a disease may be diagnosed as karmic: the effect of an incident that occurred in the past, whether in this life or a past one. This may include a circumstantial cause, for example, ill-treatment from a spouse or family member. In such a case, the healer states that the onus lies on the family and community to participate in both the healing and the necessary changes needed to promote long-term health and wellbeing. Once the family and community members have accepted this, the healer may then choose to treat the patient.

Traditional healing does not always take place in private. People often share their problems and consult the healer in a public place. Families and other community members may also actively engage in the treatment process. Traditional healers know that simply treating the person will not be enough in many cases, and that pranic healing will not affect a permanent cure unless a change in lifestyle or attitudinal change occurs. Until this happens, any improvement in mental and physical health will be short-lived. Very often, the problems for which people come to a healer are the result of unhealthy relationships within the family or community. In this situation it is imperative that all concerned parties participate in the healing process.

Use of vibhooti

There is a particular method of healing in which *vibhooti,* or sacred ash made from pure cow dung, is used. To prepare it, cow dung is burnt and made into ash. The ash is then strained through a piece of cloth. The refined ash is mixed with milk, made into balls and dried. Once dried, the balls of ash are again burnt and the procedure is repeated. This process is repeated seven, eleven or fifty-one times, according to the tradition of the healer.

Using the thumb, the vibhooti is placed at the eyebrow centre of the afflicted person. This act is accompanied by the chanting of a specific mantra. Once the chanting is complete, the preparation is blown away and the process repeated three more times. Following this, salt is placed at the space between the eyebrows and then also blown away, this time audibly and with more force.

After the healing procedure is complete, the pranic healer leaves the person and takes a walk outside. He may walk as far as two or three miles before returning to the patient. Where the healer goes and what he does is a well-kept secret, known only to initiates. It is believed to involve disposal of any toxic energy that has been cleared from the healing process.

On return the healer ascertains how the person feels. If no change has taken place, the healer sends them away explaining that no more can be done; the healer makes no pretence. If there has been a slight improvement the healer may suggest that another healer be contacted. If the person has been healed, they are asked to leave immediately and to never return to the same healer. This seemingly austere custom upholds the integrity of the healer and the power of faith and belief that is crucial for healing.

Disposal of toxic energy

It is common practice that after pranic healing, the healer must dispose of the toxic energy. This ensures the healer remains unaffected and that the toxic energy will not be transferred to another person. In India, such toxins are properly discarded under certain trees such as the banyan, peepal, tulsi or mango tree. Based on this, there is a rule that one should not urinate or sleep under such a tree. Similarly, objects that carry or contain disease are buried in the earth.

The following is a true story. The son of a rich family was digging around the foundation of his home and he found a golden statue of a snake. Thinking the gold to be valuable he kept it and melted it down. Within a few days, he fell ill with a fever and began losing weight. He was taken to the hospital and checked for cancer, tumours, blood disease, and so on; however, no cause could be found. Eventually, a priest was called who said that this was not a physical illness, but a divine punishment due to unknown causes. He was taken to a pranic healer who experienced gold radiations emanating from the boy's body. He knew nothing about the gold statue, but the amount of gold required for treatment corresponded exactly with the amount of gold that the boy had melted down. The family then told the healer about the golden snake the boy had found. It was discovered that someone had originally buried the snake because it carried a disease. Upon this discovery the father had the gold recast into a snake. The healer passed the golden snake over the boy's body, buried it again and the boy was healed.

Ancient wisdom

In order to be effective, traditional pranic healers must understand the different types of illnesses and their causes, ranging from the evil eye to karmic illnesses. Treatment generally involves various upward, downward, left, right, or circular passes with the hands or by blowing the prana with the breath. These techniques require pranic sensitivity and have to be learnt properly as with any science.

Traditional healers are not formally educated to practice their art, but learn it through apprenticeship and assisting their gurus. Quite often the knowledge is passed down within the family. Most healers require many years of purification to acquire purity of body and mind and to attain the subtlety required to work with prana. Purification practices may include rising early each morning, performing *nadi shuddhi*, purification of the nadis, while immersed waist deep in water, practising *mouna*, silence or controlled speech in order to conserve prana and observing a simple diet.

Traditionally, healers are not supposed to charge for their services. In fact, it is widely believed that if they charge for their services their healing powers will vanish. This belief relieves the healer of any selfish motive and is in agreement with the tantra shastras which state: "Neither gold nor silver, neither cloth nor food, nothing can be accepted." These days most healers have some other source of livelihood. They farm, raise cattle, have small businesses or shops and teach in schools among other things.

Traditional Indian healing methods have evolved over time and still thrive today despite their ancient origins. Throughout India, the existence of many subtle forces and forms of energy in nature is still well known by all levels of society and it is the pranic healers who preserve the wisdom and knowledge of prana that is the foundation of these ancient healing techniques.

References

[1] Dalal, Ajit K., 'Folk wisdom and traditional healing practices: Some lessons for modern psychotherapies', *Foundations of Indian Psychology*, 5–4 1, 2007.

5

Prana Pratishtha

The practices of prana vidya, as presented in this book, allow one to realize one's own pranic potential as well as extend the wealth of prana to others to bring about a positive change. The scope of prana vidya, however, is limitless. The science of prana can be used in ways that can change one's entire outlook on life and understanding of the laws of nature. For instance, the creation of artificial life has been an ongoing experiment in the scientific circles of the present age, but the ancients had possibly already mastered this art, using a variation of prana vidya. Swami Satyananda once explained in a satsang that the story of Gandhari's hundred sons in the epic *Mahabharata* is not just a story; it is an example of vedic cloning. While we no longer have access to the method that may have been used in this case, we know of the prevalence of at least one other method handed down the tradition, indicating the breadth of prana vidya. This is *prana pratishtha*, literally 'establishing prana' – infusing life into an insentient object.

Invoking the force

Prana pratishtha is one of the most esoteric vidyas and an inseparable part of tantra. Through an elaborate system of rituals, an object of worship is consecrated or charged, with the presence or power of the one whose grace will be invoked. This infusion of cosmic energy, or prana, into the object, brings it alive with subtle yet vital energy. In fact, the object, image or idol is merely a focal point for the external worship; the real essence of worship is in the power installed either by a great soul or by someone established in the practice.

The word *pratishtha* means a form that provides a firm foundation, a fixed basis, a conscious dwelling or abode for the divine power, or *shakti*. The significance of the word with regard to prana pratishtha can be found in the mantra: *Om prati-tishtha parameshvara* – "Oh Lord, abide here." In the practice, prana, which is by nature formless and unfathomable, is made to assume a form, for the purpose of bestowing grace, or an energy transmission that uplifts and expands consciousness.

The practice of prana pratishtha indicates that image worship is not intended as an indulgence in fantasy. The symbol is used as a medium for establishing communion with the cosmic energies. The images are not the idle fancies of sculptors, but shining channels through which the heart of the worshipper is directed towards the divine. Although the spiritual aspirant appears to be worshipping the image, he is actually feeling and experiencing the presence of the divine within that image. However, his capacity, predisposition and understanding define how he would imbibe that power.

Parallels in quantum physics

The principle of prana pratishtha corresponds with discoveries made in quantum physics. Scientist Izhac Bentov describes the interaction of energy between a person and a rock, an animate and an inanimate object in his book, *Stalking the Wild Pendulum.*[1] He states that if a piece of rock is kept on an altar and prayed to every day, in the course of time, that rock will come to reflect the person's energy and respond to their prayers.

What Bentov discovered through quantum physics is something yoga has long known: an interaction, a give and take of energy, can occur between animate beings and inanimate objects. This explains how and why prayers are answered, mental worries disappear and freedom and lightness are experienced at sacred places such as churches, temples and mosques. People endowed with faith and belief visit these sites. This infuses the place with energy, which in turn provides nourishment. While this process of give and take may occur naturally over a course of time (or a certain place may be naturally charged), the ritual of prana pratishtha ensures that an object of worship becomes a centre of power before the worship commences. Every act of worship performed thereafter, strengthens this force.

Channels of grace

There are various stories in the scriptures that describe how a particular individual was ordained to establish a place of worship, for the person had earned the merit to invoke divinity. In the texts of pancharatra tantra, for instance, Lord Shiva describes to Rishi Narada the need to build a place of worship to connect with the divine. Following the prescribed methods for the building of a temple, an image or statue is installed and the practice of prana pratishtha is performed. Or, in saurya tantra we find the story of Samba, Sri Krishna's son, who performs intense austerities to please the sun god to be rid of his leprosy. Surya appears before him and asks him to build a temple at a particular spot and bring priests from a specific clan, who are able to invoke the essence of fire, to conduct the worship.

Swami Niranjanananda describes the occasion where he presided over the prana pratishtha ceremony during the inauguration of an Ugra Tara temple, one of the tantric deities, in Saharsa, Bihar. The original statue had been installed by Sage Vasishtha, the guru of Sri Rama, in ancient times. Over the course of time, the temple had been ravaged by nature and the statue was completely destroyed. To revive the temple, the people of Saharsa built a new structure and a new statue of Devi in accordance with the shastras. Once the work was complete, Swami Niranjan was invited to perform the elaborate ritual of prana pratishtha in order to infuse the life force into the statue, causing it to come alive and responsive to the *bhavanas*, feelings, and prayers offered. For every sense expression, there was a corresponding mantra and a corresponding ritual; mantras were chanted for sight, mantras were chanted for smell, mantras were chanted for touch, and so forth. In this particular instance, it took fourteen hours to complete the entire prana pratishtha *vidhi* or ceremony.

The tradition maintains that prana pratishtha must be performed by a special person. It is a sadhana that invokes the power of the divine from the spirit of one's own being, from the deeper layers of one's consciousness. Therefore, the shastras say that only one who is a pure channel for the divine can perform prana pratishtha; it is only they who can invoke the paramatma from within their own heart and infuse it into the *murti*, or symbol. Such a person must be highly accomplished in mantra sadhana and possess the necessary siddhis to be capable of performing this level of energy transmission. The main instrument for prana pratishtha is the mantra, the sound vibration, of the deity. *Avahana*, invocation, including the chanting of mantras, is used to invoke the cosmic power. Once an image has been consecrated in this way, it must be worshipped in a devotional atmosphere so the energy of the deity intensifies over time.

Performing prana pratishtha

Within the ancient rituals of consecration, various symbols are used that have evolved from different philosophies. Some of the steps involved are as follows:[2]

1. The icon for worship is installed in a temple built specifically for that purpose. The building of the temple involves soil-testing, fitness of the locality, study of omens and astrological conjunctions, propitiation of site deities, and application of established architectural principles (vastu shastra).

2. Construction of the platform where the icon will be placed, its consecration, and propitiation of protective deities around the platform.

3. Preparation of the icon, including the selection of the stone for sculpting, is accompanied by rituals. When the sculptor has completed the preparation of the icon in conformity with the scriptural prescriptions, he must perform a preliminary ritual of consecration which involves mantras and offerings of sacred water, grains, cow products, food, medicinal herbs, precious stones and metals.

4. After this preliminary consecration, the icon is shifted to the site of the shrine. Before the formal and final consecration, the icon is cleansed once more by mantra, cow products and pure water. For images of human form there is another ritual; opening of the icon's eyes. Essentially this is the painting of the eyes accompanied by mantras and more offerings of grains, butter, curd and milk.

Finally, for purifying the icon and making it a fit dwelling for the divine spirit, an elaborate ceremonial bath is administered. Subsequently, the icon is shifted to another auspicious seat and is immersed in edible grains while the *Purusha Sukta* is recited. After this, the icon is treated to various rituals:

- *Tattwa nyasa*, placement of the fundamental elements on the different parts of the icon
- *Kalaa avahana*, invoking the soul and other aspects of divinity and branches of learning in the heart of the icon
- *Prana pratishtha*, infusion of vitality into the icon
- *Homa*, fire ritual.

Through the rituals of consecration, one essentially transforms the murti or image into a divine presence. It is said that once the ritual is complete, it is no longer referred to as a murti but as actual divine presence.

Consecration of Shivalingam

The ritual of prana pratishtha, in accordance with Shaiva agama philosophy, is also used to consecrate a Shivalingam rendering it fit for worship and for the performance of *abhisheka*, a sacred ceremonial bath. According to this school of thought, the infusion of energy is understood to occur at the time of the ritual joining of Shiva and Shakti, pure consciousness and the energy of primordial action. The form of a lingam represents these two aspects. The top portion of the lingam represents Shiva, that which is formless and unmanifest. The pedestal represents Shakti. During the ritual of prana pratishtha, the lingam is equipped with the pedestal, symbolizing the infusion of Shakti, cosmic energy, into Shiva, pure consciousness.

Within the sanctity of Shiva Peeth, set in the grounds of Satyam Udyan in Ganga Darshan, abhisheka is performed on the consecrated Shivalingam every month on the 5th and the abhisheka of Sri Yantra takes place every month on the 6th. These dates commemorate the mahasamadhi of Swami Satyananda and the gates of Satyam Udyan open for all to participate and be uplifted by the power of the divine. Both of these sacred forms, the Shivalingam and Sri Yantra, representing Shiva and Shakti, have been infused with cosmic energy.

Significance of mantra

While prana pratishtha refers to the actual infusion of cosmic energy, mantra is a vital part of the ritual for avahana. Mantra is chanted to invoke and awaken the divine energies. According to Swami Satyananda, the correct application of mantra is another specialized form of prana vidya. Within each individual, mantra is a subtle and unique form of prana. In tantra, the fifty letters of the Sanskrit alphabet are directly related to particular physical and psychic centres. Correct invocation of mantra will affect an energy charge in the psyche, which is then transmitted to the physical body. The power of mantra affects prana which in turn heals the body and transforms the mind. (See *Prana and Pranayama*, pp. 65–78).

Based on this intricate knowledge, gurus use and prescribe mantras for specific purposes. Transfer of prana for the purpose of spiritual awakening and healing can be accomplished by using a mantra invested with power received from a guru. Direct energy transmissions such as *shaktipat* are also bestowed on the spiritual aspirant by the guru. During shaktipat, energy is made available to the sadhaka directly through the guru who is a channel for the divine energy. It may occur through a look, through spoken words or through a formal initiation.

Visiting temples and holy places infused with the divine, participating in acts of worship, immersing oneself in the powerful vibrations of mantra, and experiencing energy transmissions from a master or guru, are imperative in the quest to evolve, to understand ourselves and the cosmos. Saints, sages and gurus continue to selflessly channel these cosmic energies in order to expand our consciousness, to create positive samskaras and to connect us with the divine.

References

[1] Bentov, Izhac, *Stalking the Wild Pendulum,* E. P. Dutton, New York, 1977.

[2] Rao, Prof S.K. Ramachandra, *Agama-Kosha Volume 9: Consecration,* Kalpatharu Research Academy, 1994.

6

Research on Prana Shakti

There has been a perceptible shift in the consciousness of humankind in the last century, as more and more people have turned towards the realm of the spirit to understand themselves and the universe. Terms like 'prana' and 'kundalini' have become part of modern dictionaries and taking leave for a meditation retreat is not unusual. At the same time, a large majority continue to ask: "How can we be sure these ideas and experiences are real? How do we know they are not hoaxes perpetrated by fraudulent individuals to gain name, fame and a quick fortune? And even if certain people really have experienced kundalini, what good is it to us? We still live within our old frames of references, with our sufferings and joys, our petty problems and trivial idiosyncrasies. Can the yogis and prophets really lead us out of our present limited modes of existence into the dawn of a more illuminating day?" Of course, questioning leads to discovery. As Albert Einstein once said, "A thought that sometimes makes me hazy: 'Am I or are the others crazy?'"

To provide an answer, there has been a movement to verify the subjective experiences of 'psychics' through the medium of science. Various individuals and institutions have conducted laboratory experiments that lend modern credibility to centuries-old wisdom. Yogis have entered Faraday cages and machines have mapped gods. Not only has this given another framework of understanding to the experiencers themselves, but it has also inspired the ordinary individual to explore a different level of reality.

Evidence of pranic body

In the 1970s the first objective evidence of the existence of the pranic body, the aura and the chakras was obtained through a study conducted by a kinesiologist, Dr Valerie Hunt, and her associates at UCLA (University of California, Los Angeles), USA. For the study, Dr Hunt developed a high frequency AuraMeter™ that was able to record the electrical energy, or aura, from the body's surface. The energy radiating from the body's atoms produced frequencies 1,000 times faster than any known electrical signals of the body and had a continuous, dynamic modulation, unlike the pulsating signals of the nervous system.[1]

Bruyere, an aura reader, assisted the study and incorporated a number of different measurements to determine the colour of the electrical frequencies. Electrodes were attached to eight traditional chakra locations and acupuncture sites, such as the eyebrow centre, *ajna chakra*, the crown of the head, *sahasrara chakra,* and the heart centre, *anahata chakra*. The EMG recorded the change in electrical activity on one track of a two-track tape recorder. Simultaneously, Bruyere recorded her description of the colour, size and activity of the auric fields on the audio track. Using a second microphone, subjects described their spontaneous experiences and images. It was quickly evident that the distinctive wave form on the oscilloscope correlated reliably with colours reported by Bruyere using her psychic sensitivity.[2]

Further research was conducted to ascertain the meaning of the five vibrational spectrums identified, and their profound emotional, psychological and behavioural effects were investigated. Studies also revealed that sound as well as colour were produced by a particular frequency of energy vibrations. The recorded sound was at a perceivable frequency and audible when amplified. Even when the sound was too low to be heard, the vibration was still felt in the soft body tissue and the hollow areas of the head, spine, chest and abdomen.

When mapping bioenergy fields in later research, Dr Hunt discovered that each individual had a unique resting pattern, and when the individual was in full health the bioenergy field was composed of balanced, coherent energy patterns across the full spectrum of frequencies. Conversely, the bioenergy fields of people who were ill or soon to become ill had either deficient or hyperactive energy patterns. This discovery reflects an underlying principle of most traditional healing systems: the state of the pranic or energy body is directly related to the state of physical health. For centuries healers have used energy vibration in the form of colour, sounds, magnets, homeopathic medicine, acupuncture and massage to bring vitality and balance to the pranic body. According to Hunt, the idea from basic biology that life forms are complex energy exchange systems is fast becoming the frontier of medicine, psychology, education and communication.

Research and development still continues at The BioEnergy Fields Foundation Mission, founded by Dr Hunt. Currently, the Foundation aims to build an enhanced AuraMeter™ System for use in medical settings. The system has the ability to diagnose illness or the predisposition to illness and to identify an appropriate treatment. Research is also underway to provide further evidence for the healing efficacy of traditional healing techniques that manipulate or alter the energetic body to heal specific diseases.

Kirlian photography

Kirlian photography was invented in 1939 by Semyon Kirlian, a Russian electrician, after he noticed a spark jumping between electrodes attached to a patient. Inspired by this discovery he went on to create a device that photographs electrical activity around objects. The device places 40,000 volts at high frequency through an electrode and into photographic paper. When an object is placed on the paper the electrical field is affected and an image is produced. The Kirlian photograph shows light emanations, flares, sparks and coronas around the object photographed. Some people believe this is a photograph of an aura, that is, a reflection of the pranic energy field chemically represented in a sensitive emulsion.

Since that time many studies have taken place using Kirlian photography. Experiments have revealed that inanimate objects such as coins have inert, stable and unchanging auras. In living things, however, the aura changes with mental, emotional and physical changes. For instance, frightened, nervous and anxious people tend to have blotchy light emanations. People in whom there is excitement, anger or loss of inhibitions usually show increased emanations.

Graydon Rixon and John Murray report the results of an interesting investigation with leaves which shows that when the tip of a leaf is cut off, the outline in the electric field remains, so the leaf appears to be intact.[3] Images of plucked leaves taken over time show that their originally brilliant flares gradually diminish in luminescence until eventually no photo can be obtained. Yogis state that prana leaves the body at death, and it could well be that these photographs are showing the death of a leaf.

In her book, *The Probability of the Impossible* (Plume Books, NY, 1975), Dr Thelma Moss describes the following research done in the United States using Kirlian photography:

1. Dr David Sheinkin and his colleagues at Rockland State Hospital, New York, have studied patients suffering from respiratory, gastrointestinal and mental illnesses. They found that the corona, or the aura, measured by Kirlian photography changes radically with different illnesses. In the future, we may be able to determine disease based on the pattern of the aura, and thus predict illness before it starts or progresses into a more serious phase.

2. Dr Moss studied Kirlian photography to examine the interchange of energy between people. One case study involved two people who were asked to look into each other's eyes until a strong connection was felt between them. Once a connection was made, both their finger pads were photographed, yet the photograph of one of the pair's finger pads was missing. This is an interesting observation with great implications for our everyday interpersonal transactions and for the studies of emotions and empathetic and non-empathetic feeling states.

3. When Dr Olga Worall, the famous American psychic and pranic healer, was photographed, she was found to have the ability to direct her energy at will. Healers have been shown to have abnormally large energy flares when compared with normal people.

In 1978, Romanian scientists reported the development of a method of body scanning they called electronography.[4] It is similar to the Kirlian method yet more sophisticated and uses a variety of recording devices ranging from black and white photography to coloured videotapes. Images are produced by varying an electromagnetic field generated by a unique high voltage field. More than 6,000 people have undergone electronography at the Labour Protection and Hygiene Centre in Bucharest and experimental studies have revealed that it is possible to detect differences between healthy and sick tissue. The light intensity varies, for example, between dark for inflammation to light for cancer. Using this technique of auric diagnosis is expected to open extensive areas in preventive and therapeutic medicine.

In recent years, at St Petersburg State Technical University of Informational Technologies, Mechanics and Optics, Russia, Dr Konstantin Korotkov has created a GDV Camera which measures the distribution of energy levels of biological objects. It is based on the Kirlian effect. Gas Discharge Visualization, or GDV, instruments use glass electrodes to create a pulsed electrical field to measure electro-photonic glow. The GDV Camera has the capacity to show normal, deficient or excess energy states, the field distribution around the human body and energy states of the chakras. While the implications may be significant, the GDV Camera reflects an estimation of the organism's current energetic state and is not intended at the present time to diagnose, treat, cure, or prevent disease.

Nadis and chakras

In terms of proving the existence of *nadis*, energy channels, and *chakras*, whirling vortices of energy, Dr Hiroshi Motoyama, President of the International Association for Religion and Parapsychology, has done considerable research. He states, "By studying a number of books about the nadis and chakras of yoga, I have been able to establish that *asana,* posture; *mudra*, gesture; *pranayama*, pranic regulation; and *dharana*, concentration, were ingeniously evolved on the basis of knowledge of the nadi system, which is equivalent to Chinese acupuncture meridian systems or channels of vital ki or chi energy."[5]

Dr Motoyama has written that acupuncture and the yogic concept of nadis have the same foundation. We are dealing with systems that have been in operation for millennia, and which have probably existed side by side for as long as man has wandered over the Eurasian land mass. This in itself is reason to believe that there must be something solid at their foundations for people to have accepted and followed their theories for so long. Systems which do not give results are usually quickly discarded. However, scientists today, in the light of modern scientific reasoning, look for models to explain these ancient phenomena so they can be accepted in today's society.

To see whether nadis really do exist or not, Dr Motoyama developed two devices that can measure the energy emitted by the body. He claims that the energy photographed by the Kirlian device is the same as that emitted from acupuncture meridians, such as in the fingertips. The first machine he calls the Apparatus for Meridian Identification or AMI. It consists of an electrode box, computer and data printout machine. Special electrodes designed by Dr Motoyama are attached to the twenty-eight acupuncture points on the fingers and toes. He then sends a small electric current of about three volts through the electrodes and records the Galvanic Skin Resistance, GSR, at each point just before and just after the body reacts to the charged voltage.

Dr Motoyama's machine is super-sensitive, able to measure minute changes in the nervous system activity within approximately one to ten microseconds. The values obtained are compared with those from over two thousand subjects. If the value is greater than a normal range, the meridian is overactive and if it is less, the meridian is underactive. One man whom he studied at Stanford University in the United States had lung cancer. Instead of the normal value of one thousand in the lung meridian, this man had a value of only one hundred and fifty, showing a great depletion of energy in that area.

Comparing the results of normal people with those who have a manifested illness and definite symptoms, provides a unique method of measuring body energy, health and the potential for disease in an individual. The value taken before the electrical charge indicates the long-term constitutional state of the body, the degree of metabolism. The value taken at the time of electrical discharge indicates the body's ability to react to a stimulus, and is also influenced by weather and climatic conditions. The value after the discharge points at the temporary functions of the body and basic tissue resistance.

Dr Motoyama uses acupuncture theory to analyze his data. For example, an abnormal lung reading may indicate abnormality in the large intestine meridian due to their yin-yang relationship. The functions of all the organs and their relationships are explained in acupuncture. According to Dr Motoyama, one can then know disease tendencies before organic disease manifests.

This is a boon for preventative medicine, enabling the healer to inform the individual of the steps he should take to avoid future problems. It will also save much time and expense for hospitals, and can avoid many unnecessary investigations. The device is already being used by a number of hospitals to screen patients, and its results are being compared to those of X-rays and biochemical tests by the Kanagawa Rehabilitation Centre in Japan. The AMI instrument is in use in some American and many Japanese medical institutions as both a diagnostic tool and for research into health and disease.

The second machine developed by Dr Motoyama is called the Chakra Machine. Some claim that this machine can directly measure the vital energy emitted from the human body without attaching electrodes. Using a specially designed pre-amplifier and lead in a copper shielded room, even the most subtle energy can be detected by the electrodes which slide up and down the frame according to the part of the body being measured. An electromagnetic field is set up between the electrodes, and when the body emits vital energy it affects the magnetic field. Dr Motoyama has diagnosed cancer using this machine, and claims to be able to record chakras in both their awakened and unawakened states. He presents the data for the claim clearly laid out in his books.[6]

In another experiment to see whether nadis and acupuncture meridians actually do exist, Dr Motoyama attached electrodes to specific points on the body, and a common electrode was placed at one end of an acupuncture meridian. No changes were noted in the electric field on the hand or in the area of the nerves corresponding to the point of stimulation. Only those specific points reacted that were said to have close correspondence with that meridian.

In yet another experiment, the arm was covered with liquid crystals which react to changes in temperature by changing colour. The source point on an acupuncture meridian was stimulated with heat and three or four minutes later the colour of the crystal along the meridian changed markedly, indicating a rise in temperature.

Psychic healing

Investigating the phenomenon of psychic energy and how it fits into psychic healing and other related subjects, Dr Hiroshi Motoyama used his AMI and chakra machines in an experiment whereby a psychic healer attempted to transmit prana into a subject. The results of this experiment were presented to the Fourth International Conference on Psychotronic Research, held in Sao Paulo, Brazil in 1979. From the experiment Dr Motoyama proposed that:

- Psi-energy, or prana, is emitted through fingers and palms.
- When this energy is injected into a chakra, changes are induced in the acupuncture meridians, or nadis, containing the point or connected to the chakra.
- The meridian system and the sympathetic nervous system are mutually related.
- The activity of the psychic or pranic energy in the meridians and that in the sympathetic nervous system proceed in opposite directions, and the entire system of the body is maintained in dynamic balance and harmony by their opposite actions.
- Psychic healers have the ability to discern disorder in the meridian system or in the body organs and tissues by feeling the psi-energy emanating from the patient.
- When psi-energy is injected into a patient in psychic healing, changes are induced in the meridians of the healer closely associated with his awakened chakra. This implies that the chakra is the source of energy.
- Psi-energy is first converted into a form of physical energy which, in turn, generates changes in physical variables.
- Excitement in the sympathetic nervous system and the cardiovascular system was noted during psi-energy transmission.
- A close relationship between nadis, meridians, prana and the sympathetic nervous system seems to exist.

- Psi-energy and physical energy have mutual interactions through the intermediary of the chakras.
- In psychic healing, the energy which generates the phenomenon is supplied by an awakened chakra and is emitted by acupuncture points at the fingertips or through the palm.

Non-touch healing

Many traditional healing systems recognize that the level and flow of energy is crucial for the proper functioning of the physical body. Energy is said to fuel the activity of the nervous and circulatory systems which are central to the functioning of the physical body. Thus, the physical body can function normally only if each constituent part is supplied with a sufficient amount of energy.

Two studies by Dr Motoyama and his associates examined the effect of non-touch pranic healing on the pranic body. This technique involves holding the hands above the body to stimulate and harmonize prana in the pranic field surrounding the body. The first study conducted in 2010 by Koji Tsuchiya and Dr Hiroshi Motoyama focused on the effect of pranic healing on the energy body.[7] Changes were measured during four sessions of pranic healing performed on a breast cancer subject. Based on an upper and lower body energy imbalance, the healing treatment aimed to cleanse and pacify the lower chakras and to energize and expand the upper chakras. The AMI results showed a distinct reversal of the upper and lower energy imbalance after treatment. The study provided the first observation of energy changes by means of an electrically measurable variable and strong objective evidence for the reality of energy manipulation claimed in non-touch energy healing.

The second study, conducted with Koji Tsuchiya and Toshiaki Harada, focused on the effects of reconnective healing.[8] Reconnective healing is a form of non-touch energy healing in which the energy of the universe works through the healer as a medium. The healer examines the condition of the patient's body and makes energetic adjustments to restore vitality and health. Reconnective healing is distinct from many other non-touch energy healing modalities in that the healer does not require any prior knowledge of the patient or any pre-planned protocol to perform the healing.

The study utilized Dr Motoyama's AMI to monitor changes in the body's energetic conditions. The purpose of the study was to see if reconnective healing could induce energetic changes detectable by the AMI and, if detectable, to evaluate the characteristics of those changes in the context of the healing.

In this particular study, the patient's legs had become emaciated following a heart operation that left him unable to walk. At the time of the operation a benign tumour was also found in the right kidney. Before the healing trial the AMI showed a significant upper and lower energy imbalance with substantial deficiencies in the lower body meridians. In addition, significant left and right imbalances were detected in the lower body. These results were found to be consistent with the particular health conditions of the patient, namely, the inability to walk for more than six months and the tumour in the right kidney.

The most essential change brought about by the healing trial was the correction of the large energy imbalance between the upper and lower body. This 'filling' of energy in the lower body, reactivated the autonomic nervous system, which then revitalized and enhanced the functioning of the lower body. The overall energy level remained essentially unchanged which suggested that, rather than receiving energy, the healing action redistributed the patient's own energy to replenish the deficiencies in the lower body. The significant left and right imbalances, which existed before the healing trial, virtually disappeared. While the study focused on revealing pranic changes, it was noted that immediately after the third healing session the subject stood up without help and walked slowly without a walker. This was not totally unexpected in view of the pranic changes described.

To venture beyond

It is only recently that science has been able to tune into the universal energy via its advances in technology. When X-rays, electrons, radioactivity and the quantum principle were discovered between the years 1895 to 1900, Nobel Prize winner Albert Szent-Gyorgy said, "None of these were, or could be, revealed by our senses. They meant that surrounding man was a world of which he had no previous inkling, about which his senses could give him no information."

The same applies to the energies being uncovered and explored by people such as Drs Hunt and Motoyama. It seems we are learning to discover more and more about the subtle levels of the energy that surrounds us, yet are beyond our sensory capacity. Dr Motoyama has said, "If it is revealed that man does not live only on energy taken from food and air, but also on a kind of psychic energy, we shall have to change our attitude and standpoint greatly toward ourselves and our existence."

From the accumulated scientific research, it seems that an instrument sensitive enough to detect the existence of prana, nadis, chakras and acupuncture meridians is becoming a reality. Humankind is moving towards an age where an explanation of previously unexplained phenomena, such as how we can heal through yoga and prana vidya, is becoming accessible to the ordinary person. Prana vidya is not new; however, it was previously only accessible to a few who were initiated into the healing science of yoga and through their own personal *tapasya*, austerities, intense effort and research into meditation, had discovered the vast untapped resources within.

Yogis, seers and healers have laid out maps by which we can raise our own level of energy and directly perceive the force of the universe. The work of researchers is helping to verify these ancient claims. However, while science may explore and make the proof of energy available via machines, we can tap the essence only by direct experience which comes from practice.

References

[1] 'Electronic evidence of auras, chakras in UCLA study', *Brain Mind Bulletin*, Vol 3, No.9, March 20, 1978.

[2] *ibid.*

[3] Murray, J. & Rixon, G., 'Kirlian Photography', *Yoga*, February, 1977.

[4] 'Russians develop dynamic Kirlian-type process', *Brain Mind Bulletin*, Vol.3, No.10, April 3, 1978.

[5] Motoyama, H., 'Yoga and Oriental Medicine', *Research for Religion and Parapsychology*, 5(i), 1 March 1979.

[6] Motoyama, H., 'The Mechanism through which Paranormal Phenomena Takes Place', *Religion and Parapsychology*, 975, 2.

[7] Tsuchiya, K., and Motoyama, H., Study of Body's Energy Changes in Non-Touch Energy Healing, 1. Pranic Healing Protocol Applied for a Breast Cancer Subject, *Subtle Energies & Energy Medicine,* 20, 2 (2010).

[8] Tsuchiya, Koji, Ph.D., Harada, Toshiaki, Ph.D., Motoyama, H., Ph.D., Study of Body's Energy Changes in Non-Touch Energy Healing, 2. Reconnective Healing Performed on a Subject Suffering from Emaciated Limbs, *Subtle Energies & Energy Medicine,* 21, 2 (2010).

Practices

7

Safeguards for Practices

Slow, steady and systematic is the way to proceed with prana vidya. The guidelines given here should be followed until the practitioner has completely mastered the practices of prana vidya at a psychic level. If these guidelines are not followed correctly, there is a high risk of incurring physical and/or mental imbalance.

Guidance: It is necessary to have guidance for the awakening of prana shakti. A guru, master or trained teacher should be present while this technique is being learned. The awakening of this energy is sometimes experienced as a terrible pain in some part of the body which suddenly shoots up to the brain. It can also be an intensely pleasurable experience.

Selflessness: Those who wish to use prana vidya for healing others must refrain from all selfish motives with regard to those they are helping. The tantra shastras state, "Neither gold nor silver, neither cloth nor food, nothing can be accepted." It is important not to expect anything in return for psychic healing.

Advice and precautions

Systematic approach: One should always move from practice to practice in the recommended order, consolidating each one steadily and systematically. Any attempt to rush the process may result in severe physical or mental imbalance, or both. It is recommended that each stage be mastered before progressing to the next. This may take one month, one year or more. (See Index of Practices for a summary of the practices for each stage of prana vidya.)

Time of practice: Prana vidya should ideally be practised in the early morning, preferably between the hours of four and six or during the hours before sunrise. At this time, the body and mind are calm and refreshed after sleep, and the pranas are balanced and ready to awaken. The practice should not be performed at night when the pranas are dissipated and unstable.

Place: Prana vidya should be practised in a calm and peaceful place where one will not be disturbed. Ideally the place of practice should be somewhat isolated, away from people, noise and interruptions. One may practise in the open air or in a well-ventilated, clean and pleasant room. One should never practise in a foul-smelling, smoky or dusty room. Avoid practising in the sun or wind. The soft rays of the early morning sun are beneficial; however, when they become stronger, they are harmful and the body will become overheated. Practising in a draught or wind may cause chills and upset the body temperature.

Posture: One may practise in a comfortable meditation posture or lying in shavasana. One may also lie on the right or left side. If one wishes to practise sitting in a chair, a cushion or stool should be placed underneath the feet, as a direct earth contact creates discharge of prana from the feet. The legs should be stretched out straight in front during the advanced practices so that no obstruction is felt in the flow of energy. If one is lying in shavasana it is necessary to place a thin padding under the head so that the neck and back of the head are comfortable. However, the padding should not be so thick that it causes the neck to bend, as this will impede the energy flow. Many of the prana vidya practices involve ajna chakra, therefore the head must be comfortable. Although the instructions are to remain still during the practice, if one has to move due to pain, one should do so without disturbing oneself, relax into the new posture, become still and then proceed.

Awareness: One should maintain awareness throughout the practice and not fall asleep. Those who find it difficult to remain awake in shavasana should practise in a sitting position with their legs either crossed or outstretched. If one is in a weakened state or very drowsy, one should do a short practice; instead of 49 rounds do 10 or 27, for instance. Ten rounds done with full awareness are very beneficial and will provide motivation to keep on practising.

Clothing: If clothing is worn during the practice, it should be loose and comfortable so there is no constriction. The clothing, blanket, pillow, mat and so forth, should all be of a natural fibre such as cotton or wool; synthetic fabrics and rubber are not good conductors of prana, therefore foam or plastic covered mats are not recommended.

Metal: Before practising one should remove all metal objects such as rings, watches, amulets, spectacles, as metal should have no contact with the skin. In prana vidya, psychic energy is concentrated and then directed like a laser beam. The practitioner can experience electric shocks during this time at the points where the body is in contact with metal.

Post-practice disorientation: One should never open the eyes or move the body immediately after completing the practice of prana vidya. It is important to first become fully aware of the external environment. This may take some time. During the practice, the consciousness enters the psychic dimension and sometimes cannot return immediately to the physical plane. If this is the case and the eyes are opened too quickly, considerable disorientation may be experienced for some time, especially after the more advanced practices. This may take the form of memory loss, lack of temporal awareness, or a general sense of disorientation. If one has this experience the solution is simple. Close the eyes and go back up to ajna. Commence ujjayi pranayama and slowly and carefully move the consciousness down to mooladhara with full concentration. Repeat this several times. Then open the eyes and check that you have fully returned to normal waking consciousness.

Returning prana from ajna: One should make sure that at the end of the practice the prana is returned to mooladhara from ajna.

Loss of personal prana: One danger in performing psychic healing on others is that prana may be lost unless one knows how to protect and replenish it. Placing oneself inside a protective symbol before sending prana out is a helpful technique at the level of pranamaya kosha. However, an individual also interacts at subtler levels. Consequently, one must have some connection to a higher source. If one reads the accounts of different psychic healers, one will find that they all had some link with a divine power. Throughout the healing process, the awareness must be maintained that 'I am not the doer.' One should try to feel oneself as an instrument for the cosmic healing energy to flow through.

Disease transfer: Many healers suffer from sickness due to transference of disease. Many benign and compassionate healers have suffered for that reason. If a psychic transference takes place, the healer must know how to remove it. If one feels oneself as the doer in any action, one attracts the karma of that action. Therefore, the healer should learn how to maintain contact with the eternal source of prana and surrender all efforts to the source.

Need for discrimination: Disease, suffering, ageing and death are all part of life and evolution. Prana vidya for oneself or others may not always be appropriate, therefore discrimination must be cultivated and applied.

8

Essential Preparation

Prana vidya is a powerful psychic technique. It is therefore important that the novice prepare slowly, carefully and under expert guidance.

The immediate aim of prana vidya is to awaken and direct prana consciously. By developing a subtle awareness you are able to perceive and gain knowledge of the nature of prana, leading to new dimensions of awareness. Prana vidya is concerned with both the expansion of consciousness and the awakening of prana, which eventually transforms into meditation and perfect union. Seen in this light, the healing aspect of prana vidya is of secondary importance. The ultimate aim is to transcend the pranamaya kosha, the bio-plasmic or light body, for then the dormant energies of the chakras and of kundalini will awaken.

Prana vidya is the culmination of many years of yoga practice. Technically it sounds simple, and it is, for those who have awakened prana shakti and evolved their awareness. However, for most people the practice is elusive. Without the basic foundation, you may practise for years and never achieve the true experience.

Preparation is essential. Before attempting the practices of prana vidya, mastery of certain yogic techniques is essential. Prana vidya requires receptivity and sensitivity to prana, proficiency in pranayama, the ability to visualize prana as well as having a thorough knowledge of the physical body. A wide range of yoga practices are recommended in order to prepare the body, mind and pranas. Success in the practice of prana vidya depends on proficiency in these preparatory techniques.

Hatha yoga

The practices of hatha yoga rank first as preparation for the prana vidya practices, firstly, for developing a steady body and secondly, for attuning the pranamaya kosha. With steadiness of body and balancing of prana, the mind automatically becomes calm and steady, and is able to achieve a higher meditative state.

Asanas remove all pranic blockages and stimulate the chakras, helping to rebalance and raise the level of prana in the different areas of the body.

Pranayama is essential to prana vidya. Ujjayi pranayama, the psychic breath, is used during the practice to facilitate the awakening, distribution and withdrawal of prana. Other pranayamas are also used to systematically purify and rebalance the nadis and awaken the prana.

Bandhas are psychic locks used to raise the level of prana and reverse the direction of pranic flow. For example, moolabandha reverses the downward flow of apana and sends it upward, while jalandhara and uddiyana bandhas reverse the upward flow of prana and send it downward. This reversal causes apana and prana to meet at samana and brings about an awakening of the prana in that area.

Mudras are gestures or practices that redirect the prana or concentrate it in one location, preventing the dissipation of energy. For example, by folding the tongue back in khechari mudra, *vishuddhi chakra*, the throat centre, is awakened. The sacral centre is stimulated by contracting the urethra and the anal sphincter muscles in vajroli and ashwini mudras respectively, awakening the energies connected with swadhisthana chakra.

Yoga nidra

The practice of yoga nidra is necessary primarily because it teaches one how to relax. One may know that the body is tense and feel stiffness or tightness in different areas, yet not know how to relax deeply. Perhaps one can relax one's muscles; however, tension still remains inside. In yoga nidra one learns how to relax at a much deeper level: not just the physical body, but the pranic body, the emotions, the mind and the psyche. When there are tensions in the body, emotions and mind, the energy flow is blocked. Depending on the amount and kind of tension, it can be so blocked that one becomes chronically ill. It is very difficult to practise prana vidya if one is in such a condition that one is unable to access the required amount of energy. Yoga nidra also teaches one to direct one's awareness to, and develop familiarity with, the different parts of the body. This is essential in prana vidya, which involves directing prana to specific body parts and organs via the psychic pathways.

Prana nidra

Prana nidra is a technique of pratyahara that works directly with pranamaya kosha. In practice it is similar to yoga nidra. In addition to bringing about a state of *pratyahara*, withdrawing of the mind from the senses, prana nidra also develops pranic sensitivity and balances or harmonizes the pranas. Both these aspects are crucial for success in prana vidya. Usually in the beginning, prana is experienced as forms of uncontrolled energy, such as tingling or sensations of warmth in the body. In prana vidya, control and direction of energy is developed, which requires the ability to perceive currents of prana flowing within the pranic body. Prana nidra develops this pranic awareness in a systematic way. Prana may be directed to the physical organs and systems; the pancha pranas: prana, apana, samana, udana and vyana; the nadis: ida, pingala and sushumna; and the chakras. Prana nidra is recommended as a preparatory practice (see Chapter 10).

Meditation

Kaya sthairyam, or body steadiness, is important, as the aspirant must be able to sit in a steady posture for some time to experience and visualize the movement of prana. Physical movement tends to break the concentration and the inner vision will be lost.

Japa is an important practice, as according to the tantra shastras, mantras have the power of healing. If the power of mantra is added to the distribution of prana, as is demonstrated in the practice in Chapter 16, the healing power of prana vidya is greatly enhanced. Only those mantras given by the guru, or universal mantras such as *Om*, *So-Ham*, the Mahamrityunjaya mantra or Gayatri mantra should be used. Gayatri is the mantra for awakening prana; for self-healing, use your personal guru mantra. Regular practice of japa and *anushthana*, prolonged mantra repetition, awakens and perfects the power of mantra.

Ajapa japa is essential for developing awareness of the nadis and breath, important keys to prana vidya. Awareness of the psychic passages and the psychic breath must be mastered so they can be used spontaneously while awakening, distributing and withdrawing prana.

Visualization and concentration practices develop the ability to perceive and experience the internal plane, which is too subtle for the external senses to grasp. In the beginning, prana vidya visualization focuses the powers of will, concentration and imagination to create a mental image of a particular part of the body or organ being infused with energy.

Chidakasha dharana is necessary because the movement of prana is visualized, not within physical matter, but within the psychic space of the body. One must develop awareness, not only of *chidakasha*, the mental space, but also of *sthulakasha*, the whole body space, an area in which the movement of prana can easily be seen.

Chakra shuddhi and tattwa shuddhi practices complete the preparation for prana vidya by purifying and awakening the chakras and the tattwas.

Kriya yoga practices utilize and channel the physical, pranic, psychic and mental forces. In doing so, these natural forces are harmonized and refined, leading to the awakening of one's own being. Subtle and direct perception is developed through kriya yoga. In this way, kriya yoga enhances the depth and experience of prana vidya.

When the preparatory and purification process has been completed, the direction of prana becomes as natural and spontaneous as breathing. (Full details of these practices can be found in *Tattwa Shuddhi, Kundalini Tantra, Dharana Darshan* and other books published by Yoga Publications Trust, Munger, Bihar.)

9

Developing the Foundations

Practice 1: Yoga nidra for developing inner body awareness
Practice 2: Developing awareness of psychic passages
Practice 3: Developing awareness of chakras
Practice 4: Developing awareness of pancha prana
Practice 5: Developing awareness of pranamaya kosha

Developing the foundations

The preparatory practices in this chapter cultivate an awareness, understanding and experience of the physical body and pranic body. The following is a short overview of each practice in relation to prana vidya.

The first practice is a yoga nidra, which develops the ability to visualize different parts of the body and includes organs and muscles within the body. In the more advanced stages of prana vidya, healing energy is distributed throughout the body, thus it is important to be able to clearly visualize the whole body in detail. As a guide for beginners, Appendix B illustrates the position of the main organs within the body; however, further study is recommended to enhance one's understanding of the physical body and the way it functions.

The second practice focuses the mind on prana and the pranic flow within the frontal and spinal psychic passageways. In prana vidya, various pranic and psychic channels are utilized to awaken and direct prana. Prana is visualized in the form of white light particles, similar to the luminous light display of sparklers, yet confined and flowing within the nadis. Initially, prana will be visualized purely based on imagination. However, in the advanced stages the actual vision and personal experience of prana is required.

The next practice deepens and refines awareness of the chakras. Throughout the practices of prana vidya, the chakras are visualized as shining points of light. They are stimulated and awakened in order to attain this clarity of vision. During this process, dormant energy is liberated and the chakras are purified.

The *pancha prana* practice directs the awareness to the unique flow of each of the five major divisions of pranic energy: *prana* or *sthula prana,* the vital energy that moves upward from the diaphragm to the throat; *apana,* the vital energy that moves downward from the navel to the perineum; *samana,* the vital energy that moves from side to side in the abdomen; *udana,* the vital energy experienced as spiralling flows of light in the extremities; and *vyana,* the all-pervading flow of vital energy. (See Appendix A for a diagram of the pancha pranas.)

In the final practice, the *pranamaya kosha* or pranic body as a whole is developed and intensified.

PRACTICE 1: YOGA NIDRA FOR DEVELOPING INNER BODY AWARENESS

Stage 1: Preparation

Remove any metal objects such as rings, watches, or jewellery.

Lie down in shavasana.

Place the legs at least hip width apart, feet falling out to the sides.

Arms are beside the body, but not touching the body.

Palms face upwards, fingers relaxed, curling naturally.

For a few moments check that the body is aligned and that the head, neck and spine are in one straight line.

Gently close the eyes and the mouth.
Let the body settle into this position and continue to make any adjustments so that the body can be completely comfortable.
Check the body for comfort and warmth.
Allow the body to become still.
Allow the floor to take the weight of the body, completely surrender the body to the floor.
Be aware of the whole body in contact with the floor.
Feel the back of the body and the sensation of touch between body and floor; from the heels to the back of the head.
Intensify this awareness.
Shift the awareness to the front of the body and notice the feeling of clothing on the skin, of any coverings resting on top of the body.
Be aware of the air on the face and other parts of the body, the hands or feet.
Feel the sensation of air coming in through the nostrils.
Let go of the sensation of touch and listen to the sounds in the external environment.
Extend the awareness as far as possible listening for distant sounds.
Now move the awareness from sound to sound. As soon as one sound is heard move on to the next, and then to the next.
Move the awareness from sound to sound, not staying with any one sound and without identifying its source.
Listen for sounds coming from all directions.
Bring the awareness closer now and listen for sounds coming from within the room.
Bring the awareness closer still and listen for sounds coming from within the body, the sound of the breath, heartbeat, digestion.
Let go of the sounds and be aware of the stillness and silence of the body.

Stage 2: Resolve

Into this silence bring to mind your sankalpa, your resolve. Repeat it mentally now three times with energy and feeling.

Stage 3: Rotation of consciousness

Prepare now to rotate the awareness around the body systematically.

As a part of the body is named, simply take your awareness to that part.

Feel it from the inside and move the awareness from part to part, keeping pace with the instructions.

The energy will follow the awareness moving from part to part refreshing and revitalizing all the different parts of the body. In this way, the awareness will be rotated around the whole body.

Begin with the right hand thumb, awareness of the right hand thumb.

Move the awareness to the first finger, second finger, third finger and the fourth finger.

Palm of the hand, and the back of the hand.

Move the awareness to the wrist, forearm, elbow, upper arm, right shoulder

To the armpit, the right side of the chest, waist, hip.

Move the awareness into the right thigh, knee, shin, calf muscle, ankle, heel, sole of the foot, top of the foot.

Bring the awareness to the big toe of the right foot, second toe, third, fourth, little toe.

Feel the energy in the whole right side of the body, whole right side of the body.

Now shift the awareness to the left side of the body.

Begin with the left hand thumb.

Check that the mind is awake and alert.

Awareness of the left hand thumb.

Move the awareness to the first finger, second finger, third finger and fourth.

Palm of the hand, back of the hand, wrist, forearm, elbow, upper arm, left shoulder.

To the armpit, the left side of the chest, waist, hip, the left thigh, knee, shin, calf muscle, ankle, heel, the sole of the foot, top of the foot.

Bring the awareness to the big toe of the left foot, second toe, third, fourth, little toe.

Feel the whole left side of the body, the whole left side.

Feel both sides of the body together, both sides of the body.

Now move the awareness to the back of the body.

Be aware of right heel, left heel, back of the right leg, back of the left leg.

Be aware of the right buttock, left buttock, lower back, middle back, upper back, right shoulder blade, left shoulder blade, point between the shoulder blades.

Be aware of the back of the neck, the back of the head.

Awareness of the whole spine from bottom to top, whole spine awareness.

Move the awareness to the crown of the head.

Shift the focus to the front of the body.

The forehead, right temple, left temple, right eyebrow, left eyebrow, eyebrow centre, the eyebrow centre.

The right eye, left eye, the right ear, left ear, right cheek, left cheek, right nostril, left nostril, bridge of the nose, tip of the nose, the whole nose.

The upper lip, lower lip, point of contact where the lips meet.

Be aware of the chin, the jawbone, front of the throat, right collarbone, left collarbone.

Right side of the chest, left side of the chest, the centre of the chest.

Upper abdomen, navel, lower abdomen, whole pelvic region.

Become aware now of the whole right leg and foot, the whole left leg and foot.

Both legs together.

The whole right arm and hand, the whole left arm and hand.

Both arms together.
Be aware of the whole trunk, front and back.
The neck, and the head.
Awareness of both legs, both arms, whole trunk, the neck and the head.
Become aware of the whole body, the whole body, the whole body.
Whole body awareness.

Stage 4: Breath awareness

Become aware of the breath moving within the stillness of the body.
The natural and spontaneous breath.
Become aware of the rhythm of the inhalation and exhalation.
Focus the awareness of the breath at the nostrils and notice the temperature of the breath.
Notice the coolness of the inhalation as the breath enters the nostrils, and the slight warmth of the exhalation as the breath exits the nostrils.
Natural, spontaneous and rhythmic breath.
On the next inhalation, imagine the breath entering through the left nostril and flowing up to the eyebrow centre.
On the exhalation, the breath flows down from the eyebrow centre and out through the right nostril.
On the next inhalation, the breath enters through the right and exits through the left.
Continue with alternate nostril breathing.
Be aware of the inverted 'V' shape created by the flow of the breath.
The breath remains natural, simply the awareness moves with the breath in and out through alternate nostrils.
Begin to mentally count the breath backwards from 9 down to 0.
Mentally repeat, 'Breathing in 9, breathing out 9, breathing in 8, breathing out 8 . . .' and continue in this way until you reach 0.

If the count is lost, begin again at 9.
If 0 is reached, again begin at 9.
Use the count to maintain awareness of the breath.
Now let go of the mental counting and release awareness of the breath at the nostrils.

Stage 5: Visualization of the internal body

Prepare now to visualize the body internally.
Do so with the attitude of a witness, like watching a movie on a screen, unaffected by the images.
First move the awareness to the head.
Go inside the head and visualize the brain, a grey-white mass floating in fluid and filling the inside of the cranium.
There are many compartments in the brain; the frontal brain lies behind the forehead, the cerebrum covers the whole crown, while at the back is the cerebellum where you can feel the pressure between the back of your head and the floor.
This area is where the spinal cord joins the brain.
In this region is the slender brain stem which is like the stalk of a flower.
At the top of this stalk is the hard, pinkish pineal gland.
Now, move a little forward under the surface of the brain to the exact centre of the head.
Located here is the pituitary gland.
Visualize it as a point of golden light.
Moving further forward, bring your awareness to the eyes.
See the white eyeballs, the transparent cornea and the dark holes of the pupils.
Go behind and see the white optic nerves connecting the eyes to the brain.
Now, go inside the ears; first the tunnel of the external ear, the silvery eardrum, then the middle ear and the inner ear.
See the auditory nerve which connects the inner ear to the brain.

Move to the mouth.
Examine the mouth, teeth, tongue and palate.
Bring your awareness to the nose and enter the nostrils with the aid of the breath.
Feel the nasal orifices that open into the back of the throat.
Move your awareness down the red throat cavity, past the larynx, which contains the vocal chords, into the trachea, the windpipe, a pink velvety moist tube or tunnel that leads to the lungs.
The trachea divides into two bronchial tubes, one leading to the right lung and the other to the left lung.
Have a look around the pink lungs.
They are comprised of air sacks which fill up as you inhale, causing the lungs to expand.
As you breathe out, these sacks empty, causing the lungs to contract.
See the brown, muscular heart in between the lungs, slightly to the left, a dynamic fleshy pump.
Inside the heart, see the heart valves opening and closing in rhythm. Letting blood flow in and out, to and from the body. Heart contracting – blood flowing out, heart relaxing – blood flowing in.
Concentrate on the heartbeat for a few moments.
Below the heart and lungs is a large flat muscle called the diaphragm, which separates the chest from the abdomen.
As you breathe in and out, watch how the diaphragm contracts downward with the inhalation and relaxes upward with the exhalation.
Feel the ribcage also expanding and contracting with the breath.
Develop awareness of the chest cavity.
Bring your awareness back to the throat and now go down the oesophagus, which is a soft, rubbery tube behind the trachea.
It carries food and liquid to the stomach.

Try to trace it with the breath down to the stomach.
Now, visualize the stomach; a loosely folded, V-shaped, muscular pouch, about the size of your fist, which expands to accommodate ingested food. When the food has been properly churned and liquefied, it is slowly ejected into the duodenum, the tube that connects the stomach with the small intestine. In the C-shaped duodenum, the food is mixed with different enzymes coming from the pancreas, a small, flat organ shaped like an arrow-head, located behind the stomach.
The food is also mixed with bile produced in the liver.
The liver is a big, brown globular organ, the largest organ in the body.
It is situated under the right side of the ribcage and diaphragm.
On the underside of the liver is the pear-shaped gall bladder, which stores bile and squeezes it into the digestive tract.
On the left side of the liver is the spleen, a soft, egg-shaped organ which contains cells to clean the body of infection.
The digested food matter enters the small intestine, which is a tube about thirty feet in length.
As it rhythmically expands and contracts the food is pushed through it.
Examine the long, purplish-grey small intestine coiled up inside the abdominal cavity.
Wrapped around the small intestine is the large intestine.
On the right side of the abdomen is the ascending colon and on the left side is the descending colon.
Connecting the two is the transverse colon, sitting on top of the small intestines.
From the descending colon the unusable food, in the form of waste matter, is stored in the rectum, a short, wide tube located in the posterior part of the pelvis.
From here it is passed out through the anus.

Inside the abdominal cavity are also the two kidneys. Purple in colour, they lie behind the waist, just below the diaphragm. The kidneys, which are about the size of your palm, filter the blood, recycling useful elements and passing out waste matter in the form of urine.

On top of the kidneys, like triangular caps, are the bright yellow adrenal glands.

From the kidneys the urine travels along attached tubes, called ureters, to a pouch situated just behind the pubic bone.

This pouch is the urinary bladder and is the shape of an inverted pyramid.

Move your awareness behind the bladder to the reproductive organs.

Women should visualize the uterus, situated behind the bladder.

The uterus is a firm, thick-walled, inverted pouch with two tubes attached to the sides.

At the end of each tube is a pink mass known as an ovary.

Men should visualize a pink, solid gland at the lower angle of the bladder, in the perineum – this is the prostate gland.

Now visualize the whole abdominal area and all the organs within it.

Practise light abdominal breathing and try to see each organ moving slightly with every breath.

Feel the organs to be full of energy and working perfectly, each one in harmony with the rest.

Visualize the upper abdomen: the stomach, liver, gall bladder, pancreas and the spleen.

Then visualize the lower abdomen: the small and large intestines, kidneys, adrenal glands, bladder and organs of elimination and reproduction.

Next, take your awareness to the back and the vertebral column which rises up from the pelvis to the brain.

It consists of thirty-three bony vertebrae placed one on top of the other.

The lowest part is the coccyx or tailbone.
Above it is the sacrum.
Further up are five lumbar vertebrae behind the abdomen.
Further up still, behind the chest, are twelve thoracic vertebrae connected to twelve ribs.
Behind the neck are seven cervical vertebrae, the top two supporting the head, allowing it to pivot up and down and side to side.
See the soft, yellowish-grey, cushion-like discs in between the vertebrae.
Visualize the muscles supporting the back and spine.
In the centre of the vertebral column there is a canal.
Within this canal lies the soft, whitish-grey spinal cord.
The spinal cord is an extension of the brain.
See all the white coloured nerves emerging from the spinal cord.
Transfer your attention to the outer extremities of the body, the arms and legs.
Try to see them from within.
Move your awareness slowly down the whole right arm from the shoulder to the fingertips.
Observe the bones, joints, muscles, blood vessels and nerves.
See the hand and fingers from within: the tiny bones, the tiny capillaries, the tiny nerve fibres.
Now, go to the left arm and observe it from within.
Move slowly down observing the bones, joints, muscles, blood vessels and nerves.
Become aware of the right leg.
Visualizing each part minutely, move your awareness slowly down the side of the thigh, the knee, the calf muscle, the ankle, until you come to the toes.
See the bones, muscles, tendons, joints, blood vessels and nerves.
Go to the left leg and examine it in the same manner: from top to bottom, slowly moving from the thigh, knee, calf muscle and ankle until you come to the toes.

Finally, become aware of the whole body from within: the head, the chest, the abdomen, the back, the arms and hands, the legs and feet, the whole structure of the body, the whole body internally.

See the whole body internally in one glimpse.

Stage 6: Sankalpa

Release the image of the inner body and become aware of the internal space.

Be aware of the quality of spaciousness and stillness.

Bring to mind your sankalpa, the positive resolve made at the beginning of the practice.

Repeat it mentally three times with faith and with conviction.

Feel the sankalpa permeating the entire inner space.

Stage 7: Ending the practice

Let go of the sankalpa and once more become aware of the natural breath.

Feel the breath in the abdomen.

Be aware of the incoming and outgoing breath.

Notice the flow of breath moving within the physical body.

The abdomen rises on the inhalation and falls on the exhalation.

Feel the whole body in the chosen relaxation posture.

Be aware of the body in contact with the floor, from the heels up to the back of the head.

Be aware of the space surrounding the body.

Recall the room in which you are, the orientation of the door and windows, the colour of the walls, your position within the room.

Become aware of the sounds in the environment and allow the awareness to externalize.

The practice of yoga nidra is now complete.

Keeping the eyes closed, become aware once more of the whole physical body and prepare mentally for movement.

Take the awareness to the fingers and toes.

Slowly start to move the fingers and toes.

Gently move your head from side to side.
Take a deep breath in and stretch the arms above your head.
When you are ready, slowly sit up.
If you wish, practise palming and then gently open your eyes.

Hari Om Tat Sat

PRACTICE 2: DEVELOPING AWARENESS OF FRONTAL AND SPINAL PSYCHIC PASSAGES

Stage 1: Frontal psychic passage

Settle the body in a comfortable meditative asana.
Allow stillness and steadiness to develop in the physical body.
Become aware of the breathing process and let your awareness flow with the breath.
Be totally attentive to every incoming and outgoing breath as your breathing becomes slow and rhythmic.
Take your concentration to the breath in the throat and observe it becoming deeper.
As you breathe in, count slowly to five and as you breathe out, count slowly to five.
The breathing is effortless and natural.
Relax more and more with each breath.
Leave this practice and return to normal breathing.
Internalize your awareness and imagine a thin transparent stream of light running in a straight line between the throat and the navel; try to visualize it.
If you find this difficult, visualize instead a transparent tube, or you can picture it as having a colour such as silver or white.
Visualize it mentally without incorporating breath awareness.
Begin to move your awareness very slowly up the inside of the tube then bring it slowly and evenly down again.

Now, add breath awareness.

Let your awareness flow with the breath up and down this psychic passage.

As you breathe in, breath and awareness flow slowly and evenly up from the navel to the throat and as you breathe out, breath and awareness flow down smoothly and evenly from the throat to the navel.

Two forces are moving together in the psychic passage; the breath is the vital force and the awareness is the mental force.

These two forces constitute your being, and they are moving together within a path of power.

Now, become aware of a third force.

The awareness is moving with the breath and, along with these, the prana is also moving.

The awareness, breath and prana are moving together, up and down the psychic passage.

The prana moves in the form of streaks or particles of light.

Visualize particles of white light flowing up and down this nadi as your consciousness travels up and down with the breath.

Observe this slender flowing river of white light, the prana, flowing with the breath and consciousness.

Stage 2: Spinal psychic passage (sushumna nadi)

Now, leave awareness of the frontal psychic passage and transfer your awareness inside the spinal psychic passage.

This runs up through the centre of the spinal passage between mooladhara and ajna chakras and connects all the chakras together.

Develop the awareness of this nadi extending from the perineum, just below the base of the spine, to the mid-brain, or visualize a similar transparent, white or silver tube spanning this area from top to bottom.

Move your awareness very slowly up inside the passage.

When you reach the top, slowly bring it down again.

Try to visualize its full length from within.

Add the breath and let your awareness flow with the breath up and down this nadi.

As you inhale, try to feel the breath moving from mooladhara below the base of the spine, to ajna chakra at the top of the spine.

As you exhale feel the breath descend back down to mooladhara.

Come closer and closer to the breath, total and unbroken flow of the breath; prana and awareness are moving together up and down the spinal passage. Become aware of the prana, the particles or streaks of light, flowing along the length of the spinal passage with the breath.

Do not miss a single breath.

Stage 3: Ending the practice

Release the awareness of the psychic passage and the movement of prana.

Focus on the natural breath moving in and out of the body.

Feel the physical body surrounding the breath.

Be aware of the whole body in the chosen meditative posture.

Feel the floor beneath the body, and the space surrounding the body.

Recall the details of the room.

Be aware of the external environment, the sounds around you, smells or odours from within the room, any tastes in the mouth.

When your consciousness is fully externalized, gently and slowly open your eyes.

The practice is now complete.

Hari Om Tat Sat

PRACTICE 3: DEVELOPING AWARENESS OF CHAKRAS

Stage 1: Preparation

After making yourself comfortable in the position of your choice, commence ujjayi pranayama and begin to develop awareness of your body.

Feel the body becoming still.

Concentrate only on body stillness; the body is completely steady and motionless.

Become aware of the body as a mere shell of skin with nothing inside.

Slowly develop the experience of the body as a shell.

Complete awareness of the stillness and emptiness that you can feel within the body.

Stage 2: Awareness of the chakras

Within the stillness of the body, become aware of the spinal passage.

Visualize the passage flowing from the perineum, just below the base of the spine in mooladhara chakra, rising up to the crown of the head, to sahasrara chakra.

Intensify your awareness of this passage or visualize a transparent, silver-white tube extending all the way from the base of the spine to the crown of the head; awareness of a thin transparent stream of light from mooladhara to sahasrara.

The major chakras are situated along this nadi like tiny lights, sparkling diamonds or rubies strung on a thread.

Take your awareness to the lowest point, the mooladhara chakra, from where this psychic passage emanates.

Mooladhara is situated slightly inside the perineum midway between the scrotum and anus in males, and on the posterior side of the cervix in females.

Visualize mooladhara as a point of bright light.

Move up to swadhisthana chakra, situated at the base of the spinal column at the level of the coccyx or tailbone.

Visualize it as a point of intense light.

Move up to manipura chakra, situated directly behind the navel on the inner wall of the spinal column.
Visualize it as a point of radiant light.
Move up to anahata chakra, situated directly behind the centre of the sternum in the spinal column.
Visualize it as a point of shining light.
Move up to vishuddhi chakra, situated in the cervical plexus, directly behind the throat pit.
Visualize it as a point of vivid light.
Move up to ajna chakra, situated at the very top of the spinal column, directly behind the eyebrow centre in the region of the medulla oblongata. Visualize it as a point of gleaming light.
Move up to bindu at the top of the back of the head, where brahmins wear the tuft of hair.
Visualize it as a point of blazing light.
Finally, take the awareness to sahasrara at the crown of the head.
Visualize it as a region of luminosity.
Visualize all the chakras simultaneously.
Become aware of the consciousness ascending the spinal passage from mooladhara to sahasrara with the breath, passing through each of the chakras in turn.
As you breathe in, the breath comes up from mooladhara, along the spinal passage, piercing all the chakras.
By the time you have completed the inhalation the awareness should have reached sahasrara.
As you begin to exhale the awareness should be at sahasrara.
When you complete the exhalation the awareness should again be at mooladhara.
There is control over inhalation and exhalation; the awareness moves with the speed of the breath.
At the time of inhalation, the awareness moves up from mooladhara and passes through swadhisthana, manipura, anahata, vishuddhi, ajna and bindu to sahasrara.

At the time of exhalation the awareness moves down from sahasrara and passes through ajna, bindu, vishuddhi, anahata, manipura and swadhisthana to mooladhara.

As you pass through the various points of light, mentally repeat the names of the chakras.

Begin the process of inhalation at mooladhara and, as the breath and awareness pierce each chakra, repeat the name of the chakra: mooladhara, swadhisthana, manipura, anahata, vishuddhi, ajna, bindu, sahasrara.

Then exhaling, repeat: sahasrara, bindu, ajna, vishuddhi, anahata, manipura, swadhisthana, mooladhara.

Continue moving the awareness and the breath through each chakra point with mental repetition of their names.

Be completely aware of the process. It should not be unconscious; apply total concentration.

Continue with the practice, intensifying the awareness of the chakras.

Stage 3: Ending the practice

Now get ready to end the practice.

Leave the awareness of the spinal passage.

Leave the awareness of the chakras and of the ujjayi breath in the spine.

Gradually become aware of the physical body and of the surrounding physical environment.

Feel the contact of the floor beneath the body and the space surrounding the body.

Become aware of all the sounds around you.

Be aware of the sense of smell, the sense of taste.

Make sure you are totally back in your physical body.

When you feel ready, slowly begin to move the body and when you feel completely externalized, you may open your eyes.

Hari Om Tat Sat

PRACTICE 4: DEVELOPING AWARENESS OF PANCHA PRANA

Stage 1: Inner space

Lying down comfortably in shavasana, commence ujjayi pranayama and begin to observe the body.

Develop an internal experience of the body; examine yourself from the inside.

This internal viewing does not produce the same experience as when you view yourself from the outside.

When you observe the body from the inside, you are aware of the space contained within.

You are not visualizing your nose, eyes, ears, hands or arms, rather you are observing the space within the body.

Surrender the whole body to the floor as you develop and intensify the awareness of inner space.

Be aware of the whole body from the top of the head to the tip of the toes.

Experience the space in the whole body as one unit.

It is not awareness of localized space, not *chidakasha*, the mind space, or *hridayakasha*, the heart space; it is awareness of *sthulakasha*, the space throughout the body.

Intensify the awareness further, being aware of the body as a whole.

Stage 2: Breathing through the pores

Along with observing the space within the body, become aware of the natural and spontaneous flow of breath.

As you breathe in, feel that the whole body is breathing in, not through the nostrils, but through each and every pore and cell.

As you exhale, experience the breath being expelled through each and every pore. Experience the whole body breathing through the pores and the cells.

With the next inhalation, begin to introduce the experience of physical expansion.

With the exhalation, begin to experience physical relaxation; feel all the muscles relax.

As you breathe in, sthulakasha, the inner space, expands, as you breathe out this space contracts.
Observe the phenomenon of the body feeling like it is expanding and contracting like a balloon.
Intensify this awareness and remain awake and alert.

Stage 3: Vyana awareness

Now, begin to develop the awareness of pranic energy pervading each and every part of the body.
If you can have a visual experience, it is better.
Try to see the space contained within the body as being filled with countless small points of light moving rapidly in every direction, causing streaks and streams of white light to shoot throughout the body.
The entire body space is filled with this light.
This is a very subtle experience; to perceive it you must intensify your concentration and awareness.
If you succeed, well and good. If you do not succeed at first, keep on trying; do not be disheartened.
Continue to experience streaks of light moving in random patterns in every direction, something like the effect of waving many sticks of lit incense in the dark.
This is *vyana chaitanya*, awareness of vyana, the prana that pervades each and every part of the body and acts as a reserve force for the other individual pranas.

Stage 4: Udana awareness

Now, direct your attention to the extremities: the arms, legs and head. This aspect of prana, located in the extremities, is called udana.
First become aware of your legs.
Experience the energy moving at great speed around the legs in circular patterns, spirals or rings of light.
This energy moves from the hips to the toes.
Be aware of the legs and the udana prana in the legs.
Visualize circular forms of energy in the legs.
Intensify this awareness.
Do not sleep. Remain alert.
Next, bring your awareness to the arms.

Experience the same circular energy in the arms, it is moving in spirals from the shoulders to the fingertips.
Intensify this awareness.
Try to visualize circular patterns of udana prana or rings of light covering the arms.
Then come to focus at the head.
Experience rings of udana prana rising from the throat to the top of the head. Develop *udana chaitanya*, awareness of the udana prana, in the extremities of the body.

Stage 5: Samana awareness

Now become aware of the energy in the abdomen between the navel and the ribcage. The prana in this area is called samana.
See this energy moving horizontally from one side of the waist to the other and then back again; the movement is very rapid.
Develop *samana chaitanya*, awareness of samana, the prana localized in the abdomen.
See samana as light streaking from left to right and from right to left at great speed.
Intensify this awareness.

Stage 6: Apana awareness

Your awareness now shifts down to the energy known as apana, located in the lower abdomen between the navel and the perineum.
Here you will visualize the downward moving force of apana prana, as streaks of light moving from the navel to the perineum, filling up the whole lower abdomen with downward moving waves of light.
Develop *apana chaitanya*, awareness of apana, the energy that moves downward in the lower abdomen, in the form of light waves.

Stage 7: Prana awareness

Finally, bring your awareness to the energy in the chest region.
This energy is known as prana, and it moves upward from the diaphragm to the throat.

Visualize light waves moving upward from the navel, filling the whole chest with light.
Develop *prana chaitanya*, awareness of prana, the energy moving upward in the chest region.
Intensify this awareness.

Stage 8: Ending the practice

Now stop this practice of prana chaitanya and begin to externalize the consciousness.
Very slowly, begin to become aware of the external environment: the sounds, your breathing process, the gross physical body, the floor and where the body is touching the floor, the people around you, the room and the different objects in the room.
Slowly and gently move the toes, the fingers, the legs, the arms and the head from side to side.
Take a deep breath in and stretch the arms over your head, stretching the whole body. Release the breath.
Then slowly sit up, keeping the eyes closed.
Do not open the eyes immediately; let normal consciousness return to each and every part of the body.
When the mind is completely extroverted, slowly open your eyes.

Hari Om Tat Sat

PRACTICE 5: DEVELOPING AWARENESS OF PRANAMAYA KOSHA

Stage 1: Preparation

After making yourself steady and comfortable in your position, begin to relax your whole body.

Gently close your eyes and watch the breath in the nostrils.

Relax all the muscles in the physical body.

Feel your body becoming totally at ease.

There is no tension or tightness in any limb or part.

Surrender completely; feel as if you are floating on an ocean of peace; soothing waves lap over your body.

See light and energy shimmering all around you.

Surrender yourself completely to this protective aura of light.

Bring your awareness inside and develop the experience of space within the body.

Look inside the body and see nothing but empty space.

The skin of your body is like a shell and inside, from head to toe, there is nothing but a void.

Gaze into this inner void.

Develop the awareness of space; the space which comprises your individual being.

Stage 2: Expansion and contraction of the inner space

Become aware of the breath.

Begin to practise slow, deep breathing.

Move your awareness in and out with the breath.

As you develop awareness of each breath, begin to experience that you are breathing not only through the nose, but also through each and every pore and cell of your body.

Begin to breathe with the whole body; feel your whole body breathing evenly as one unit.

Now leave the awareness of the nasal passages, lungs and chest, and breathe only through the pores.

Experience every pore and cell of the whole body breathing.

Continue to breathe for some time through every pore and cell of your body. Imagine they are opening and closing as you breathe in and out.

As you breathe in through every pore, try to feel that the whole inner space of your being is expanding outwards in every direction; the whole inner space from head to toe is increasing in size.

As you breathe out through every pore, experience this inner space contracting evenly on all sides.

Use the power of your imagination and try to actually feel your whole body breathing, and to see it expand and contract.

As you take a deep breath in, feel that the breath is entering through every pore and cell of your body and that the whole inner space is expanding like a bubble.

Then, breathe out slowly through every pore, and experience the inner space contracting.

Intensify this experience of the growing and diminishing, the expansion and contraction of inner space.

Stage 3: Visualization of pranamaya kosha

Along with the experience of expansion and contraction of the inner space with the breath, become aware of prana in the form of light pervading this space.

With each breath, the inner space becomes filled with particles of white light moving in all directions at a great speed, forming streaks within the space.

Begin to see this body of light.

As you inhale, this light body expands.

As you exhale, this light body contracts.

Concentrate your awareness fully on the experience of the light within you expanding and contracting with each breath.

The light field you are experiencing is your pranamaya kosha moving to the rhythm of the breath.

Continue with this practice until the field of light of the pranamaya kosha fades.

Stage 4: Ending the practice

Get ready to slowly end the practice.

Leave the visualization of the body of light.

Let go of the experience of breathing through the pores.

Leave the awareness of the empty space within the body and come back to *annamaya kosha*, the gross physical body.
Focus at the nose tip and feel the breath entering and leaving the nostrils.
Become aware of all external sounds.
Slowly move the fingers and toes; move the head gently from side to side.
Stretch the arms over your head.
Only when you are externalized and totally back in your physical body, sit up and open your eyes.

Hari Om Tat Sat

10

Prana Nidra

The practice of prana nidra is designed to bring the experience of the energy body, or *pranamaya kosha,* to our conscious awareness. Pranamaya kosha represents the vital energy that animates the physical body, the *annamaya kosha,* and vitalizes the mind, the *manomaya kosha*. Prana moves continuously throughout the body in autonomous and often rhythmic patterns, fuelling the vital systems of the body and mind. The conscious mind, that part connected with the frontal lobes of the brain, often does not actively monitor these energies. Another part of the mind, the unconscious part connected with the primitive, ancestral part of the brain, continuously monitors this life-giving and life-maintaining system of prana.

It is possible to train oneself to be more consciously and distinctly aware of prana and the pranamaya kosha by practising various yogic techniques such as pranayama, yoga nidra and prana nidra. As a result of achieving greater awareness, one can further explore, and ultimately better manage, this dimension of the personality.

Awareness

Rather than inundating the conscious mind with data about pranamaya kosha on an intellectual level where it will remain theoretical, the aim of the practice of prana nidra is to expand the awareness and experience of prana to previously unconscious areas. In a technique similar to yoga nidra, the awareness is systematically directed to various forms, levels and experiences of prana.

In both yoga nidra and prana nidra one experiences, at increasingly subtle levels, things about oneself of which one was previously not aware. One relaxes the physical body, the annamaya kosha, in shavasana or any other relaxation posture. One relaxes the energy body or pranamaya kosha, through the breath. One relaxes the mental body, the manomaya kosha, by awakening the experience of opposite feelings or memories. One awakens the vijnanamaya kosha, the intuitive sheath of knowledge, through the use of symbols, and the anandamaya kosha, the inner awareness of bliss, by encouraging deeper and deeper states of relaxation while maintaining the witnessing awareness. When relaxation is complete, receptivity is greater.

In yoga nidra and prana nidra the consciousness is in a state between waking and sleep, yet it is subject to neither. In this state, the mind is exceptionally receptive. While the mind is open and receptive, yoga nidra brings the deeper layers of the psyche into the conscious experience and prana nidra brings increasingly subtle experiences of prana into the awareness. Sage Patanjali's *Yoga Sutras* state that we can become steady in wisdom through knowledge gained during the processes of sleep and dream (1:38): *Svapna-nidra-jnana-alamban* – "Or else (the mind can be made steady) by giving it the knowledge of dream and sleep for support."

Pranamaya kosha

Prana nidra is similar to yoga nidra in both purpose and technique. They both access knowledge directly by opening previously unconscious layers of the mind. The main difference is that prana nidra is more specialized. It deals with four main types of experience: i) the flow of energy in the pancha pranas, ii) the flow of energy in the nadis, iii) the flow of energy in the chakras, and iv) the expression of these energy flows, particularly at the levels of vitality, feelings and emotions.

As one learns to recognize, manage and direct these energy components, one becomes aware of new levels of one's being. The aim of prana nidra is to make one's awareness of oneself more extensive and more subtle. It allows one to experience:

- The connection between annamaya kosha and pranamaya kosha and thus to become aware of vitality and energy flows throughout the physical body. In this way prana nidra is useful as a physical therapy. The connection between manomaya kosha and pranamaya kosha, the mental states and the energy level or vitality. This can happen when one witnesses different types of thoughts, attitudes and feelings giving different 'voltages' of energy. Therefore, prana nidra is useful as a mental therapy also.
- The structure and function of the pranamaya kosha itself: the pancha pranas, nadis and chakras. New understanding of how one's personality relates to the external world results from experiencing the energy flows in ida and pingala nadis. Different experiences arise when specific chakras receive different 'voltages' of energy through one's concentrated awareness. Whole new perspectives on life open up as the *granthis*, the psychic knots that bind one to specific modes of dealing with life, are released. Thus, prana nidra is useful in establishing new habits, perspectives and lifestyle.
- The connection between pranamaya kosha and vijnanamaya kosha: the connection between balanced energies and the rise of intuitive knowledge. This knowledge allows one to understand and act spontaneously, in harmony with the situation, rather than having to crosscheck everything through the intellect. Prana nidra is useful in providing the courage to let go of conditionings and simply live one's dharma.
- A fusion of pranamaya kosha with anandamaya kosha, the ocean of bliss. Therefore, it is useful in establishing

atmabhava, the spiritual outlook on life which allows one to feel the unity with all and recognize all beings as equal.

Guidance

The guidance of guru is necessary for one to progress beneficially in any yogic practice, particularly those that lead to deep introversion, and this guidance should be followed so that the enhanced energy and awareness are used for the welfare of all.

In order for the experiences of prana nidra to remain manageable and progress harmoniously, it is advisable to maintain a healthy diet as well as a regular practice of shatkarmas, asana, pranayama and simple mudras. These practices purify and cleanse the body, mind and pranas. Simple yoga nidra and antar mouna can be regarded as complementary practices, and should be practised steadily before practising the more intense aspects of prana nidra such as the chakra shuddhi techniques. Conversely, prana nidra can help one to engage in the more subtle practices of any meditation technique, including prana vidya and tattwa shuddhi.

Stages of prana nidra

The stages in prana nidra are similar to yoga nidra; however, in prana nidra one keeps bringing the awareness back to pranamaya kosha. All of the following components, from stage one to five, are included in each session. The selection from stage four is dependent on the needs and capabilities of the student. The stages are as follows:

1. Establish *kaya sthairyam*, body stillness, in shavasana or any other relaxation posture where the spine is straight and the body can remain comfortable and motionless.
2. Introduce witnessing sounds and other sensory phenomena, thoughts and the breath, perceiving them as energy.
3. Rotation of consciousness in body parts, focusing on energy shifts and awareness of vitality.

4. Awareness of prana associated with the breath in any of the following ways:
   - Parts of the body: limbs, organs or systems
   - Pranayama, such as natural abdominal breathing and mental nadi shodhana
   - One or more of the pancha pranas: prana, apana, samana, udana and vyana, including their direction and intensity
   - Expansion and contraction of the pranic body
   - Exploration of the nadis, especially ida and pingala nadis
   - Exploration of the chakras
   - Chakra shuddhi
   - Tattwa shuddhi.
5. Conclusion: carefully externalizing the awareness and bringing the attention back to annamaya and manomaya koshas.

Two introductory practices are given:

PRACTICE 1: AWARENESS OF PRANAMAYA KOSHA

Stage 1: Preparation

Please get ready for the practice of prana nidra.

Before beginning the practice, remove any metal objects and adjust the clothing.

The best position is shavasana; however, you can use any other relaxation posture you can hold comfortably, without moving for 20 to 30 minutes.

Settle the body into your chosen position.

Take time to become comfortable, with the back and neck straight, limbs, stomach and face relaxed, eyes and mouth gently closed.

Be sure you will be warm/cool enough for the whole practice.

Stage 2: Relaxation

Feel the solidity of the body as it settles on the floor, and let it become still.

Feel the body. Be aware of the skin covering the body.
Be aware of the clothing and any covering on the body.
Check the body and make any adjustments so you can remain still and comfortable for the duration of the practice.
Be aware of any sensation in the head, neck, shoulders, the whole spine, in the chest, abdomen, the whole trunk of the body, legs, feet, whole body.
The physical body should be so comfortable that it doesn't disturb you at all, and you can become aware of the more subtle energies of pranamaya kosha.
Become quiet and alert, aware of the subtle energies throughout the body.
Feel the breath in the nostrils, and be aware of the temperature of the breath.
Feel fresh energy flowing in as you breathe in, and relax as you breathe out.
Natural, spontaneous breath, but with awareness in the nostrils, aware of energy coming in as you breathe in, and relaxing as you breathe out.
The body is so still you can clearly feel the movement of the breath and the energy associated with the breath.

Stage 3: Rotation of consciousness

Now be aware of the whole body.
Aware of the whole physical body and its contact with the floor, and we will begin to rotate the awareness around the body.
As a part of the body is named, feel it from the inside, feel the energy in each part of the body and as you move the awareness from part to part, the energy will follow the awareness, refreshing and re-energizing all the different parts of the body.
Begin with the right hand thumb.
Be aware of the whole thumb, from the tip to the base: the shape, the bones and joints, the energy inside.
Move the awareness to the first finger.
Feel the energy flowing from the thumb and filling the whole of the first finger, right to the tip.

Move the awareness to the second finger and feel the energy flowing right up to the tip, third finger, fourth.
Palm of the hand, the warmth of the energy in the palm of the hand.
Move the awareness to the back of the hand and let your awareness and the energy flow up through the wrist, forearm, elbow, upper arm, shoulder.
Feel the energy in the shoulder, armpit, the side of the chest, waist, hip. Move the awareness into the right thigh and feel the energy throughout the thigh, knee, shin, calf muscle, ankle, heel, top of the foot, sole of the foot.
Feel the energy, the sensitivity in the sole of the foot, the instep.
Bring the awareness to the big toe of the right foot, second toe, third, fourth, little toe.
Push the energy right down into the little toe of the right foot.
Feel the energy in the whole right side of the body. Notice that the right half of the body feels more alive, invigorated or maybe even bigger than the left side.
Now we will move the energy throughout the left side of the body.
Begin with the left hand thumb.
Be aware of the whole thumb, from the tip to the base: the shape, the bones and joints, the energy inside.
Move the awareness to the first finger, feel the energy flowing with the awareness, filling the whole of the first finger, right to the tip.
Second finger, third finger, fourth.
Palm of the hand, feel the warmth of the energy in the palm of the hand. Let it flow to the back of the hand, wrist, forearm, elbow, upper arm, shoulder.
Feel the energy in the shoulder, armpit, the left side of the chest, waist, hip, the left thigh, knee, shin, calf muscle, ankle, heel, the top of the foot, the sole of the foot.
Feel the warmth of the energy, the sensitivity in the sole of the foot, the instep.

Bring the awareness to the big toe of the left foot, second toe, third, fourth, little toe.
Be sure energy is saturating the little toe of the left foot.
Feel the energy in the whole left side of the body.
Feel both sides of the body energized, balanced.
Now we will begin to move the awareness and energy throughout the back of the body.
Be aware of all the toes, the toes of both feet, move the awareness like a wave of energy up through the heels, calf muscles, backs of the knees, backs of the thighs, buttocks, the curve of the back, the back of the shoulders, back of the hands, back of the arms, back of the neck, back of the head, the whole back of the body.
Be aware of the whole head.
Be aware of a slightly different quality in the energy here.
Awareness to the top of the head as though there is a subtle vibration at the top of the head, whole head relaxed, the forehead relaxed, left eyebrow, right eyebrow, eyebrow centre.
Feel the right eye, become aware of the right eye and let it relax, feel the small muscles around the eye and let them relax.
Feel the left eye, become aware of the left eye and let it relax, feel the small muscles around the eye and let them relax.
Feel the energy of the eyes.
Be aware of the eyebrow centre.
Feel the point between the two eyebrows.
Hold the awareness there for a while and feel a little pulse of energy. Lightly touch that point with your awareness.
Then let the awareness and energy slide down the bridge of the nose to the nose tip.
Be aware of the right nostril, and feel the breath moving inside the right nostril.
Feel the temperature of the breath as it moves in and out of the right nostril.

Just for a couple of breaths, feel the energy moving in with the breath as you breathe in, and relaxing, letting go of nervous tension as you breathe out.

Feel the left nostril, feel the temperature of the breath as it moves in and out of the left nostril.

Feel the energy moving in with the breath as you breathe in, and relaxing, letting go of nervous tension as you breathe out.

Now practise with both nostrils, feeling the energy moving in with the breath as you breathe in, and letting nervous tension, mental tension, discharge from the body as you breathe out.

Awareness of the right ear, the outside part of the ear and the inside part, the whole right ear.

Awareness of the left ear, the outside part of the ear and the inside part, the whole left ear.

Aware of the energy of the ears, open and receptive.

Move the awareness to the mouth, feel the energy of the mouth.

The upper lip, the lower lip, the whole mouth relaxed.

Chin and jaw relaxed.

Whole face relaxed, whole face relaxed, letting the whole face relax.

Now, moving the awareness and the energy down through the front of the body.

Aware of the whole face, throat, collarbones, shoulders, the whole right arm and hand, the whole left arm and hand.

Feel the whole chest, and the gentle movement of the chest with the breath.

As the lungs and rib cage expand on the inhalation, there is pressure on the diaphragm that separates the rib cage from the abdomen. Breathe in and feel the energy and chest expanding.

As you breathe out, feel everything relaxing.

The lungs and whole rib cage relax and the pressure is released as the air leaves the lungs through the throat.

Feel this process for a few breaths.

Now feel the whole abdomen, and the gentle movement of the abdomen with the breath.
Feel the diaphragm pushing down on the stomach as you breathe in, so that the navel rises.
Feel the navel fall as you breathe out and the stomach settles back.
Be aware of the energy expanding and relaxing in the solar plexus.
Move the awareness and energy to the hips, pelvis, the groin, the tops of the thighs, the tops of the knees, the shins, the tops of the feet.
Feel the whole front of the body.
Awareness of the whole front of the body from the top of the head to the toes.
Awareness of the energy emanating from the front of the body, from the whole front of the body, from the back of the body, from the whole right side, from the left side, from the whole body.

Stage 4: Breath awareness

Be aware of the natural flow of the breath.
Feel it in the nostrils.
Remain awake and just be aware of the natural flow of the breath.
Feel the energy flowing in with the breath at the time of inhalation, and then use the awareness to draw the energy up to the eyebrow centre.
Feel a distinct flow of energy going in through both nostrils and flowing upward to the eyebrow centre as you breathe in.
Feel it flowing from the eyebrow centre through both nostrils as you breathe out.
The energy rides the breath, but you can also feel the movement of the energy distinct from the breath; through both nostrils the energy flows to the eyebrow centre on inhalation and from the eyebrow centre out through both nostrils as you exhale.

The whole area of the face, head and brain are revitalized as you breathe in and the energy reaches the eyebrow centre and disperses.

As you breathe out, feel any tiredness, strain, mental tension flowing out. Continue.

Now leave this practice and begin to feel the natural breath entering the lungs.

Feel the breath flowing in through the nose and down into the lungs.

The breath goes straight in from the nose and down through the throat and into the lungs, but now the energy can be directed with your awareness.

Be aware of the long inhalation through the nostrils, the throat, into the lungs, and the expansion of the whole chest.

Feel the relaxation on exhalation.

Be aware of the breathing process for some time and feel the energy moving inside the breath in the chest region.

Feel the movement of the rib cage with the breath.

Feel the subtle, rhythmic expansion and relaxation of the lungs with the breath.

Feel the heart beating in its cage.

Feel the long rhythms of the breath and the shorter pulses of the heart beat.

Now alter the perspective a little.

Feel as though you are breathing in directly through the heart, and energy is filling the heart and whole chest and refreshing your emotions.

When you exhale, feel as though you are exhaling directly from the heart, letting go of emotional tension, tiredness and heartaches.

Practise for some time with full awareness of the energy flowing in and out with the breath in the chest region.

Now shift the awareness and feel the energy in the whole abdomen and the gentle movement of the abdomen with the breath.

Feel the diaphragm pushing down on the stomach as you breathe in, so that the navel rises.

Feel the navel fall as you breathe out and the stomach settles back.
Now, change the perspective a little.
As you breathe in, feel the stomach rising and feel the energy coming straight in through the navel centre.
On exhalation, feel as though you are breathing out directly from the navel.
Be aware of the energy expanding and relaxing in the whole stomach area. Feel the whole solar plexus being revitalized.
Feel the digestive power increasing, feel yourself able to digest anything you experience.
Feel the energy, the power of the breath in the abdominal area for some time.
Now let go of the breath and become aware of the whole body.
Feel the shape of the whole body, and begin to experience the whole body breathing, the whole body is full of energy.
As though you are breathing through the pores of the skin, be aware of the whole body breathing.
Feel a slight expansion of energy as you breathe in through the very pores of the skin.
Feel the body relaxing back to its normal dimensions as you breathe out. Feel the energy body expanding a little away from the physical body, extending past the skin as you breathe in, and letting the energy field relax back into the body as you breathe out.
You can feel it or you can see it.
Continue for some time.
Remain relaxed, not changing anything, just observing.
Be aware that you are sensing more subtle energies of your body, your vehicle.
Be aware that you are observing more subtle aspects of who you are, and feel yourself revitalized and refreshed, physically, mentally and emotionally.

Stage 5: Ending the practice

Now, from awareness of the energy body, return the awareness to the physical body.

Be aware of the shape and solidity of the physical body.

Be aware of the room in which you are practising, and any people in the room.

Be aware that you have been practising prana nidra.

Be aware of the time of day by listening to the sounds with the attitude of a witness.

Be aware of any taste in the mouth, any fragrance you can smell.

Be aware of how you are feeling physically, mentally and emotionally.

Be aware of the physical body in the relaxation posture of your choice, aware of the solidity of the body, the position of the limbs, the back, the head.

Feel the contact between the body and the floor, all the points of contact between your body and the floor.

Whole body awareness.

Check that you are fully awake and aware of the whole body.

Take a couple of slightly deeper breaths and slowly begin to move the body.

Gently move the fingers, move the toes, move the head from side to side.

Stretch the whole body as though you are just waking up in the morning. If you wish, flex the back a little.

If you are in shavasana, roll on to one side and come slowly up to a sitting position.

Keep the eyes closed.

Feel the whole body relaxed and the energy stable and refreshed.

The practice of prana nidra is complete.

Practise palming, rubbing the palms of the hands together until they feel hot and then placing them gently over the closed eyes, feeling the energy soaking into the eyes.

Hari Om Tat Sat

PRACTICE 2: AWARENESS OF PANCHA PRANA

Stage 1: Preparation

Please get ready for the practice of prana nidra.

Before beginning the practice, remove any metal objects and adjust the clothing.

Settle the body into shavasana and make any necessary adjustments.

Take time to arrange the body comfortably, with the back straight, arms away from the sides of the body, and the feet apart.

Be sure you will be warm/cool enough for the whole practice.

Stage 2: Relaxation

Feel the solidity of the body as it settles on the floor.

Make any adjustments so you can remain still and comfortable for the duration of the practice.

Be aware of the clothing and any covering on the body.

Be aware of the skin covering the body.

Feel the warmth and energy of the body on one side of the skin, and the space on the other side.

Be aware of any sensation in the head, neck, shoulders, right arm, left arm, whole spine.

Be aware of any sensation in the chest, the right side of the chest, the left side of the chest, the whole chest, be aware of the energy of the chest.

Be aware of the upper abdomen, the lower abdomen, the whole abdomen, the energy of the abdomen.

Be aware of the whole trunk of the body and any sensations there.

Be aware of the whole right leg and foot, the whole left leg and foot, aware of the whole body.

Once more, check the whole body and make any last minute adjustments, and then make a sankalpa to remain still for the entire practice of prana nidra.

The physical body should be so comfortable that it doesn't disturb you at all, and you can become aware of the more subtle energies of pranamaya kosha permeating the body.

Stage 3: Breath awareness

Now bring the awareness to the breath in the nostrils.

Feel the breath in the nostrils, and be aware of the temperature of the breath.

Feel the difference in the temperature of the breath as you breathe in and out.

Each time you breathe, feel fresh energy flowing in as you breathe in, and relax as you breathe out.

Feel tension and toxins being discharged effortlessly as you breathe out.

Continue. Be aware of the natural spontaneous breath in the nostrils, and become consciously aware of energy coming in as you breathe in, and relaxing as you breathe out.

Stage 4: Rotation of consciousness

Now be aware of the whole body.

Feel the whole physical body resting on the floor and prepare to rotate the awareness around the body.

As a part of the body is named, feel it from the inside, and move the awareness from part to part, keeping pace with the instructions.

The energy will follow the awareness moving from part to part, refreshing and revitalizing all the different parts of the body.

Begin with the right hand thumb.

Be aware of the whole thumb, from the tip to the base, the energy inside, and also the energy emanating a little beyond the thumb.

Be aware that there is warmth and energy emanating a little way all around the thumb.

Now smoothly move the awareness to the first finger.

Feel the energy flowing with the awareness, filling the whole of the first finger, right to the tip.

Move the awareness to the second finger and feel the energy flowing into the second finger right up to the tip, third finger, fourth.

Palm of the hand, feel the energy emanating from the palm of the hand, feel the warmth of the energy in the palm of the hand.
Move the awareness to the back of the hand and, as though you are shining a warm lamp into the arm, let the energy flow to the back of the hand, wrist, forearm, elbow, upper arm, shoulder.
Feel the energy in the whole shoulder.
If the shoulder is tense, let it relax.
Be aware of the armpit, the side of the chest, waist, hip.
Move the awareness into the right thigh and feel the energy throughout the thigh, knee, shin, calf muscle, ankle, heel, the top of the foot, the sole of the foot.
Bring the awareness and energy right down into the big toe of the right foot, second toe, third, fourth, little toe.
Push the energy right down into the little toe of the right foot.
Feel the energy in the whole right side of the body.
Notice that the right half of the body feels more alive and invigorated.
Be aware of the energy all throughout the right side of the body.
Now switch the awareness to the left side, to energize the left side of the body.
Bring the awareness to the left hand thumb.
Be aware of the whole thumb, from the tip to the base, the energy inside, and the aura of energy emanating a little beyond the thumb.
Move the awareness to the first finger, feel the energy flowing with the awareness, filling the whole of the first finger, right to the tip.
Let the energy flow to the second finger, third finger, fourth.
Become aware of the hand, the warmth of the energy in the palm of the hand.
Let it flow to the back of the hand, wrist, forearm, elbow, upper arm, shoulder.

Feel the energy in the shoulder.
Let the whole shoulder relax, let the muscles relax, let go of any tension. Move the awareness to the armpit, the side of the chest, waist, hip.
Feel the energy throughout the left thigh, knee, shin, calf muscle, ankle, heel, the top of the foot, the sole of the foot.
Feel the energy move into the big toe, second toe, third, fourth, little toe.
Push the energy right down into the little toe of the left foot.
Be sure you are awake and aware of energy right down to the little toe of the left foot.
Feel the energy in the whole left side of the body.
Feel both sides of the body energized, balanced.
Now we will begin to move the awareness and energy throughout the back of the body.
Be aware of the heels, calf muscles, backs of the knees, backs of the thighs, buttocks, the curve of the back, the back of the shoulders.
Be aware of the whole spine, from the base of the spine, move the awareness along the natural curve of the spine, right up the back of the neck.
Feel the back of the arms, back of the hands, back of the head.
Be aware of sensations in the whole back of the body.
Be aware of the whole head, whole head relaxed.
Awareness to the top of the head.
Awareness of the forehead, the forehead relaxed.
Feel the curve of the left eyebrow, the right eyebrow.
Become aware of the eyebrow centre and a distinct pulse of energy there.
Become aware of the right eye and let it relax, feel the small muscles around the eye and let them relax.
Feel the left eye, become aware of the left eye, feel the small muscles around the eye and let them relax.
Feel the energy of the eyes.

Be aware of the nose tip, left nostril, the right nostril, both nostrils.
Feel the energy moving in with the breath as you breathe in, and relax as you breathe out.
Be aware of the sensitivity of the nostrils, feeling the energy moving with the breath as you breathe in and as you breathe out.
Awareness to the left ear, the outside part of the ear and the inside part, the right ear, outside, inside, aware of the energy of the ear.
Be aware of the mouth, the upper lip, the lower lip, the teeth and the tongue, relaxed in the mouth.
Chin and jaw relaxed.
The energy of the mouth.
Whole face relaxed, whole face relaxed, letting the whole face relax.
Now, move the awareness and the energy down through the front of the body.
Aware of the whole face, throat, collarbones, shoulders, whole right arm, and the energy in the palm of the right hand.
Feel the whole left arm, and the energy in the palm of the left hand.
Feel the whole chest, and the gentle movement of the chest with the breath.
Feel the lungs and ribs, and the energy expanding as you breathe in, then relax as you breathe out.
Be aware of the whole abdomen, and the gentle movement of the abdomen with the breath.
Feel the energy in the solar plexus glowing a little with energy as you breathe in, like a fire glows more brightly when you blow on it. Relax as you breathe out.
Feel the hips, pelvis, the groin, the thighs, the knees, the shins, the tops of the feet.
Awareness of the whole front of the body from the top of the head to the toes, and be aware of the energy emanating from the front of the body.

Then be aware of the whole back of the body and the different quality of energy emanating from the back of the body.

Feel the energy permeating and emanating from the whole body.

Stage 5: Pancha prana awareness

Now bring the awareness to the breath.

Be aware of the flow of breath in the nostrils, and the energy riding the breath.

The breath goes straight in from the nose and down through the throat to the lungs.

Be aware of this for a few breaths.

Now on the next inhalation, draw the energy and awareness up to the eyebrow centre.

Feel a distinct flow of energy going in through both nostrils and flowing upward to the eyebrow centre as you breathe in.

Then feel it flowing out from the eyebrow centre through both nostrils as you breathe out.

Often we are not aware of the energy, it just rides the breath, but now feel the energy coming in, distinct from the breath, through both nostrils to the eyebrow centre on inhalation, and moving out from the eyebrow centre out through both nostrils as you exhale.

The whole area of the face, head and brain is revitalized as you breathe in and the energy reaches the eyebrow centre and disperses.

As you breathe out, feel any tiredness, strain, mental tensions flowing out.

Continue for 15 breaths.

Now discontinue this practice.

Prana: Be aware that the pranamaya kosha, the energy body, has five main regions of vital forces.

Prana occupies the region between the diaphragm and the throat.

Move the awareness down to the diaphragm.

Feel a subtle force moving up from the diaphragm

through the chest region to the throat.
Irrespective of the inhalation or exhalation, this force moves up.
Be aware of this flow of energy for some time.
This is the flow of prana in the upper part of the body.

Apana: Now become aware of apana.
Apana has a downward flow from below the navel down to the groin.
Take the awareness to the navel.
Feel a subtle force moving down from the navel to the perineum.
Irrespective of the inhalation or exhalation, this force moves down.
Be aware of this flow of energy for some time.
This is the flow of apana in the lower part of the body.

Samana: Now become aware of the energy in the region of the navel.
Samana is the field of energy between the fields of prana and apana.
It's very dynamic and controls digestion.
The energy here moves from side to side, like the swing of a pendulum from right to left and back again
Watch the flow of samana for some time.

Udana: Now take the awareness from samana and become aware of the limbs of the body.
Feel the whole right arm.
From the right shoulder, udana circles around the right arm, a spiralling flow down the whole right arm, from shoulder to fingertips.
Move the awareness into the right arm, from the shoulder to finger-tips and feel udana encircling it.
Now move the awareness to the left arm from the shoulder to fingertips.
Udana encircles the whole left arm, a spiralling flow down the whole left arm from shoulder to fingertips. Feel it.
Move the awareness to the right leg.

The whole right leg from groin to the tips of the toes, encircled by the spiralling flow of energy of udana.
The energy is there, just feel it.
Now, be aware of the left leg, the energy inside, permeating it and encircling it, the spiralling flow of energy of udana.
Now move the awareness to the neck and throat.
Be aware of the neck and head.
Here also the udana moves, flowing upwards from the base of the neck to the top of the head, a subtle, moving current of spiralling energy.
Feel it for some time.
Move the awareness and the energy will follow the awareness.
Keep the awareness in the region of the neck and head and feel the energy of udana there.

Vyana: Now behind these four pranic fields, like a backdrop, is the basic energy of the whole body. The whole body is permeated by the integrated and integrating field of vyana energy.
Vyana pervades the whole body. It is the background force, like a template on which the other energies move.
Feel the whole body, the whole body full of energy and light.
It is a dynamic, contained, field of energy.
Be aware of the whole body. You may feel a slight expansion of energy as you breathe in and feel the body relaxing back to its normal dimensions as you breathe out.
Continue for some time.
Relaxed, not changing anything, just observing the vyana energy field.
Feel your energy revitalized and refreshed by the focused attention of your awareness.
Feel yourself rejuvenated, physically, mentally and emotionally.

Stage 6: Ending the practice

Now from awareness of the energy body, return the awareness to the physical body.

Be aware of where you are and be aware that you have been practising prana nidra.

Be aware of the room in which you are practising, and the position of your body in the room.

Listen to the sounds with the attitude of a witness.

Be aware of any scents, of the taste in the mouth.

Be aware of how you are feeling.

Be aware of the physical body in the relaxation posture of your choice.

Be aware of the solidity of the body, the position of the limbs, the back, the head.

Feel the contact between the body and the floor.

Feel all the points of contact between your body and the floor.

Feel the energy in the body and the hardness of the floor.

Whole body awareness.

Become ready to end this practice.

Begin to move the body.

Gently move the fingers, the toes, the head from side to side.

Make sure you are completely externalized.

Flex the back a little and come slowly, smoothly up to a sitting position.

The practice of prana nidra is complete.

If you wish, practise palming, and when you are ready, gently open the eyes.

Hari Om Tat Sat

11

Awakening and Circulating Prana

AWAKENING PRANA IN MANIPURA

Practice 1: Merging prana and apana

CIRCULATING PRANA

Practice 2: Circulating prana in chakras and psychic passages
Practice 3: Ajapa japa with prana visualization
Practice 4: Circulating prana in pingala nadi
Practice 5: Circulating prana in ida and pingala

Awakening prana in manipura

The prana at *manipura chakra*, the energy centre located in the spine directly behind the navel and associated with solar energy and vitality, is awakened when the two opposing forces of prana and apana merge at samana. The *Vijnana Bhairava Tantra* says (v. 64):

> वायुद्वयस्य संघट्टादंतवाार् बहिरंततः ।
> योगी समत्वविज्ञानसमुद्गमनभाजनम ॥

> From the fusion of both vayus (prana and apana) inside or outside (the body), the yogi attains equilibrium and becomes fit for the proper manifestation of consciousness.

Prana is normally an upward moving force situated between the navel and the throat, and apana is normally a downward moving force between the navel and the perineum. However, they can be controlled and directed through tantric and yogic practices. There are numerous methods to achieve this (see *Prana and Pranayama* pp. 55–56). In prana vidya, the direction of the opposite moving forces of prana and apana are reversed with the help of breath, concentration and visualization. This is the first practice covered in this chapter.

Circulating prana

The second section focuses on the nadis to awaken and deepen the experience of prana. Prana is directed through various pranic passageways, namely the ida, pingala and sushumna nadis. The awareness and direction of prana through the nadis begins and ends at mooladhara chakra, the seat of kundalini. Circulation of prana with the force of concentration generates enormous amounts of energy. Movement of the awareness and the breath, as well as concentration and visualization of prana, purifies the nadis and chakras and develops more subtle perception. This leads to harmony and alignment between the koshas. When this alignment takes place, one crosses the threshold from outer to inner experiences. These techniques must be practised for some months until an actual experience of prana is awakened.

AWAKENING PRANA IN MANIPURA

PRACTICE 1: MERGING PRANA AND APANA

Stage 1: Preparation

Sit or lie down, ensuring that you are completely comfortable.

Adjust the position of your body so you will not have to move for the duration of the practice.

Make sure there is no tension in the body or lumps in your blanket.

If you are wearing anything tight, loosen or remove it.

Remove any metal objects you may be wearing.

Now begin to relax the whole body mentally from head to toe.

Slowly move your awareness through all the different parts to check for and release any remaining tension: head, facial muscles, neck, shoulders, back, chest, abdomen, arms, hands, buttocks, legs and feet.

Stage 2: Inner space

Once the body is calm and relaxed, internalize the consciousness and observe the body from within.

Do not visualize the body in terms of the muscular system, the skeletal system or the internal organs.

Try to develop awareness of the body in the form of space, complete emptiness. Experience the body as being a hollow shell; inside there is only space.

Go on developing the awareness of space in each and every part of the body, right down to the tips of the fingers and toes.

See this space contained within the body.

Experience the subtle inner space.

Feel yourself to be physically void.

Direct your awareness systematically through each and every part of the body and become aware of total space: awareness of the right leg and the space within the right leg; the left leg and the space within it; the right arm and the inner space; the left arm containing only space; the whole trunk of the body and the emptiness within the trunk; the head and the inner emptiness contained within the head.

Go on developing homogeneous awareness of the space contained within the body.

Stage 3: Visualizing pancha prana

Become aware of vyana, the energy which pervades the whole body.

Feel or visualize vyana in the form of streaks of light moving rapidly throughout each and every part of the body, pervading it entirely from head to toe.

This should be a process of instant visualization and feeling.

Keep your awareness internalized and intensify the state of concentrated awareness.

Continue to experience vyana, the all-pervading pranic energy, in the form of particles of light darting at random throughout the entire body. Try to feel this prana in the form of very subtle movement throughout the whole body.

Now become aware of udana in the extremities of the body: the legs, the arms, the neck and the head.

Have a vision of this prana in the form of spiralling rings of energy or circles of light, moving clockwise.

Develop awareness of udana from the hips down to the toes, from the shoulders down to the fingertips, from the throat to the top of the head.

Visualize these circles of energy moving at great speed in a clockwise direction.

Intensify this experience; have an instant visualization, instant feeling, instant awareness of the continuous spiralling movement of energy in the extremities of the body.

Now, concentrate on samana in the region of the upper abdomen between the diaphragm and the navel.

Visualize the energy in samana moving in a sideways direction.

Experience waves of light travelling from left to right and from right to left of the waist like a fast shuttle on a weaving loom.
The feeling and visualization should be instantaneous.
Intensify this awareness and visualization.
Leave samana and become aware of apana, the energy moving in the lower abdomen from the navel to the perineum.
Experience apana as waves of light energy moving downward.
Now synchronize this movement of pranic light with the breathing process.
At the time of inhalation, see the light travelling downward from the navel to the perineum.
At the time of exhalation, reverse the flow of energy and send it back upward to the navel.
Intensify the awareness of this pranic movement with the breath. While inhaling, experience the downward movement of apana; while exhaling, reverse the flow and send the energy back up to the navel.
Now become aware of prana, the movement of energy in the chest region from the diaphragm to the throat.
Experience it as waves of prana moving upward and filling the whole chest with light.
Begin to synchronize the rhythm of the natural breath with the movement of this energy.
As you inhale, follow the upward movement of the prana from the diaphragm to the throat.
During exhalation, reverse the flow and send it downward, from the throat to the navel.
A wave of light is shooting upward during inhalation and downward during exhalation.
Be aware of this pranic movement.
Intensify the awareness of prana.
Be sure to maintain your concentration without a break.

Stage 4: Merging prana and apana at manipura using exhalation

While synchronizing the movement of prana with the breath, also become aware of the movement of apana.

Each time you inhale prana moves upward and apana moves downward. Visualize and feel these two forces moving away from each other during inhalation.

At the time of exhalation both pranic flows are reversed: prana moves downward from the throat to the navel and apana moves upward from the perineum to the navel.

See and feel these two forces coming together and meeting at the navel on the exhalation, and see and feel them move apart on the inhalation.

Have total awareness of the two distinct movements of prana and apana: during inhalation, these forces move away from each other; at the time of exhalation, they merge at the navel, at samana.

Now begin to feel a strong and powerful impact as these two energies collide.

Each time prana and apana meet at the navel centre feel heat and light building up at the solar plexus, the centre of prana.

Continue this process for some time.

Maintain total awareness of the movement of prana and apana at the time of inhalation and exhalation without a break in concentration.

Experience the two waves of light energy separating and meeting with an explosive force in the region of the solar plexus.

At the time of their collision, experience increasing heat being generated in the solar plexus, there may be a physical experience of tingling at the navel.

Practise for up to 27 breaths.

Stage 5: Ending the practice

Now get ready to end the practice.

Allow the awareness of the pranas to slowly dissipate.

Be aware of the breath.
Again become aware of your physical body.
Feel the weight of your body on the floor.
Externalize your awareness.
Experience all the external sounds.
Be aware of the room in which you are lying, of any objects or other people around you.
Slowly move your fingers and toes, your hands and feet.
Gently move your head from side to side.
Take a deep breath in and stretch your arms over your head.
When you are sure that you have regained complete awareness of your physical body, slowly sit up and open your eyes.

Hari Om Tat Sat

Practice note: To familiarize with and attain greater control of the movement of prana and apana, one may practise directing these forces in several different ways. The breath may also be utilized in different ways. One may achieve the merger of the two forces on the inhalation (instead of exhalation as in the above practice) and experience them moving away from each other on the exhalation. One may experience them as moving in tandem in the same direction (for instance, both moving downwards on the inhalation and upwards on the exhalation) and then reverse the flow of one of them to create the fusion. However, it is advised that at the beginning one follows one practice for a length of time to attain mastery.

PRACTICE 2: CIRCULATING PRANA IN PSYCHIC PASSAGES

Stage 1: Preparation

Sit in a comfortable meditation posture with your hands in either chin or jnana mudra, and with the head, neck and spine straight.

You may also sit in a chair or lie in shavasana.

Relax the body completely, making sure there is no tension or tightness of any kind.

Make the body totally still like a statue.

Be fully aware of the motionlessness of the whole body as one unit.

Focus on the breathing process and relax deeply into each breath.

Tell yourself that you will not move throughout the practice.

Stage 2: Inner space

Once the whole body has become motionless and completely relaxed, internalize your awareness and observe the body from inside.

Imagine your body is totally hollow, absolutely empty.

Develop the sensation of void within the body, as if you are only a shell of skin with nothing inside.

Enter the head and see only an empty shell.

Move your awareness inside the trunk of the body.

There is nothing to be found.

Similarly, the arms and hands, the legs and feet, contain nothing but space.

Develop this experience of subtle void within the whole physical body as one unit.

Stage 3: Chakra location

Within this subtle void visualize the psychic passage of sushumna.

See it as a thin, transparent, white or silver flow of energy running from mooladhara chakra straight up to ajna chakra.

Strung on this thread of luminous light are the chakras, brilliant points of power.
As you locate each chakra, name it mentally and see it glowing: 'mooladhara, swadhisthana, manipura, anahata, vishuddhi, ajna'. You may also be able to feel a gentle throbbing sensation.
Come back down: 'ajna, vishuddhi, anahata, manipura, swadhisthana, mooladhara'.
Finally, at a glance see all these bright points glowing together like stars hanging on a fine, transparent thread.

Stage 4: Visualizing pathways on either side of the spine

Focus the awareness at mooladhara for a few seconds.
Visualize a pathway that curves like a single bow on the right hand side of the spine from mooladhara all the way up to ajna chakra.
It enters ajna from the right hand side.
This is not sushumna nadi nor is it pingala nadi.
See it curved like a bow equal in length to your spine.
Take your awareness back down to mooladhara and visualize a similar pathway that curves on the left-hand side of the spine forming a bow all the way up to ajna.
It merges into ajna from the left hand side.
This is also not sushumna nor is it ida nadi.
See it curved like a bow equal in length to your spine.
See both these passages together on either side of the spine forming two equal and perfect bows merging in mooladhara and ajna chakra.

Stage 5: Introducing ujjayi pranayama

Once you have a clear idea of these two passages, you can begin to ascend and descend along their two curves, synchronizing your awareness with ujjayi pranayama.
Begin the subtle practice of ujjayi in the throat and gently fold the tongue back into khechari mudra.
Take your awareness to mooladhara for a few seconds.
Then, as you breathe in with ujjayi, let your awareness follow the curved bow on the right hand side of the spine.

Synchronize the movement so that when your inhalation is complete, your awareness has reached ajna chakra, entering it from the right hand side.

Hold your awareness and the breath at ajna for a few seconds.

Then exhale with ujjayi as you allow your awareness to slip down following the curve on the left hand side of the spine.

Synchronize the movement so that when exhalation is complete your awareness has reached mooladhara chakra.

Practise this for some time.

Upon inhalation your awareness travels up the right hand curve from mooladhara to ajna.

Upon exhalation it travels down the left hand curve from ajna to mooladhara.

Intensify your awareness of these two curved paths, one on the right or pingala side and the other on the left or ida side.

Stage 6: Adding visualization of prana

Now, along with the awareness of the ujjayi breath, begin to visualize a stream of white, pranic light moving rapidly along these two bow shapes.

As you breathe in from mooladhara, see the white light ascend on the right to ajna in one single curve.

As you breathe out, see the light descend down the left from ajna to mooladhara in one single curve.

Go on rotating your awareness up the right, pingala side and down the left, ida side, observing this unceasing flow of intense pranic light.

After each inhalation, hold your awareness and breath at ajna for a few seconds.

Feel yourself begin to merge in this awareness of breath, consciousness and prana ascending and descending in streams of light.

Go on until the whole movement becomes spontaneous and perfectly synchronized.

Continue with ujjayi pranayama, although you may relax khechari for some time if necessary.

Stage 7: Changing direction

When this movement and visualization is harmonized and clear, reverse the order and begin to ascend up the left, ida side and descend down the pingala side.

Start at mooladhara and let your awareness curve left, following the bow on the left hand side of the spine.

Synchronize the movement so that you reach ajna on completion of the inhalation.

Hold your awareness and breath at ajna for a few seconds.

Then exhale as the awareness curves down the right hand side.

Synchronize the movement so that you reach mooladhara on completion of the exhalation.

Practise this for some time.

Intensify your awareness of this process.

Then begin to visualize the stream of pranic light moving in sequence.

As you breathe in from mooladhara see the prana ascend up the left to ajna.

As you breathe out from ajna see the light descend down the right to mooladhara.

Go on rotating your awareness up the ida side and down the pingala side, observing this continuous stream of brilliant light.

After each inhalation, hold your awareness and breath at ajna for a few seconds.

Intensify this practice.

Merge with this triple awareness of breath, consciousness and prana until you become effortlessly one with it.

Stage 8: Ending the practice

Now gently withdraw your awareness from this practice.

Again, become aware of the hollow space of your body now filled with light and subtle energy.

Let your breathing return to normal.

Become aware of your physical body and its position.
Listen to all external sounds and mentally reconstruct the outside environment.
Slowly and gently move your toes, your feet, your fingers, your hands and your head from side to side.
Take a deep breath in and, raising your arms over your head, stretch the whole body.
When you have fully regained awareness of your physical body and the external environment, open your eyes and slowly sit up.

Hari Om Tat Sat

PRACTICE 3: AJAPA JAPA WITH PRANA VISUALIZATION

Stage 1: Preparation

Sit in a comfortable meditation posture and close your eyes.
Make sure the spine is erect, the head straight and the hands on the knees in chin or jnana mudra.
Relax yourself both physically and mentally.
Become conscious of the natural incoming and outgoing breath.
Take your awareness to the breath at the throat.
Begin to breathe more slowly and deeply so that while breathing in you can count up to five, while breathing out again you can also count up to five.
Although the breath is slow and deep, it is also natural.
Increase your concentration at the centre of the throat.
Feel that each breath is moving in through the throat as if there is a small hole in the front of the throat through which you are sucking in air.
Continue this slow, deep breathing until you feel the breathing process change spontaneously into ujjayi breathing.
Be aware of the steady, soft snoring of the breath which sounds like the gentle hiss of steam gradually being released from a pressure cooker.

The tongue also folds back into khechari mudra so that the tip touches the back of the throat and the lower surface presses against the upper palate.

Ujjayi and khechari are practised together.

If the tongue becomes tired, release it for a short time and then fold it back again.

Stage 2: Psychic passage visualization

Begin to develop the experience of the body as being an empty shell, complete awareness of the inner void.

Simultaneously be aware of the stillness that you can feel within the body.

Within this stillness, become aware of the nadi which runs inside the spinal cord.

See the nadi from the base of the spine to the mid-brain; try to visualize it as a transparent, white or silver tube, luminous and bright, rising up through the centre of the spinal cord.

Inhale with ujjayi and move your awareness up through the centre of this nadi from mooladhara to ajna.

Exhale with ujjayi and move your awareness back down from ajna to mooladhara.

Continue moving the awareness together with the breath up and down the spinal passage.

Try to feel that the breathing process is taking place inside the psychic passage.

Your full awareness is focused within the passage.

Intensify your awareness of the breath, synchronized with consciousness, moving up and down the length of this passage.

Stage 3: Visualizing the pranic flow

Develop awareness of the prana flowing with the breath.

As you inhale with ujjayi breathing, watch the energy flow upward in the form of white light particles.

When you reach ajna, begin ujjayi exhalation and watch the energy flow downward in the form of light particles.

Continue this for a few minutes, like a child watching a sparkler moving up and down; see the energy flowing.

Experience the movement of pranic light.

Use imagination or memory to visualize a stream of light particles like the sun shining on a clear stream of water, or bright sparklers being moved quickly through the air.

Visualize the energy moving up and down the spinal passage with the ujjayi breath.

As the ascent and descent become steady, become aware of the chakra junctions situated within the spinal column.

Feel that the prana is piercing each psychic centre in turn, but do not try to name the chakras or stop at any particular point.

Keep the awareness moving up and down with the breath; simply be aware of each junction as you pass through it.

You are now observing the chakras strung along the spinal passage, the movement of the breath and the movement of the prana in the form of moving light.

Intensify this awareness.

Visualize the movement of prana and experience the prana piercing the chakra points one after another, like a needle threaded on the string of your own awareness.

Stage 4: Introducing the mantra *So-Ham*

Now, leave any effort to see the chakras and concentrate on the sound of the breath as it ascends and descends the psychic spinal passage.

Become aware of the mantra *So-Ham*, the subtle inherent sound of the breath.

During inhalation hear the sound 'So'; during exhalation hear the sound 'Ham'.

Observe the flow of prana as a stream of light particles moving upward to the soft sound of 'So' and downward to the equally subtle sound of 'Ham'.

Continue with this practice for some time.

Completely merge the consciousness with the movement of prana and the *So-Ham* mantra.

Full awareness of the movement of prana along the spinal passage threaded on the *So-Ham* mantra and the ujjayi breath.

Become one with the movement of the ujjayi breath.

Unite with the repetition of the mantra *So-Ham* as the breath ascends and descends.

Merge with the flow of prana that you experience in the form of a stream of white light and the vibration of *So-Ham*.

Stage 5: Ending the practice

Now stop this practice, release khechari mudra and switch back to normal breathing. Leave awareness of the psychic passage and the mantra *So-Ham*.

Focus on the breath and feel the breath moving inside the body.

Become aware of the gross physical body.

Slowly begin to externalize your awareness.

Listen to the sounds around you.

Visualize the environment around you and see yourself motionless in your meditation posture.

Make sure you are totally back in your physical body.

Check the senses, the sense of taste, sense of smell, sense of touch, sense of hearing.

Then, slowly begin to move your fingers and toes, gently move the arms and legs, and move your head from side to side.

Stretch the whole body, take several deep breaths, then carefully sit up keeping the eyes closed.

Open your eyes only when you are sure the mind is fully extroverted.

Hari Om Tat Sat

PRACTICE 4: CIRCULATING PRANA IN PINGALA NADI

Stage 1: Preparation

Assume a comfortable position either sitting up or lying down.

If lying down, preferably adopt the posture of shavasana, although you may also lie on your right or left side, as you can in most of the practices.

If sitting up, make sure your body is relaxed.

The spine should be erect, the head straight and the hands on the knees in chin or jnana mudra.

The eyes and the mouth should be gently closed.

Get ready to begin.

Become aware of the physical body and the position of the physical body.

Make yourself completely steady and still and feel your body weight to be perfectly balanced on each side.

Be completely relaxed and at ease as you observe the body becoming motionless.

There is no physical movement whatsoever; the whole body is immobile like a statue, and without tension.

Bring your awareness inside the body.

Become aware of the body as if it is a shell of skin.

Inside the body is just empty space.

Become aware of this void inside your body.

Look into the space; be totally aware of this space.

Within this space, visualize your spine.

In the centre of the spinal cord, see the transparent or silvery-white nadi and the chakra points strung along it like shining jewels on a thread.

Stage 2: Tracing the route of pingala nadi

Now we shall begin to develop awareness of pingala nadi.

Do not try to synchronize the movement of the breath with pranic movement in this practice.

Starting at mooladhara chakra, begin to trace pingala nadi: first it curves to the right and then enters swadhisthana chakra from the right.

It leaves swadhisthana from the left and enters manipura chakra from the left.
It leaves manipura from the right and enters anahata chakra from the right.
It leaves anahata from the left and enters vishuddhi chakra from the left.
Finally, it turns to the right and enters ajna chakra from the right.
From ajna begins the descent: the descending path leaves ajna from the right and crosses through vishuddhi.
Then it curves to the left and crosses through anahata.
Next it curves to the right, crossing through manipura.
From manipura it curves around to the left through swadhisthana.
Finally, it curves to the right and comes back to mooladhara from where it began.
Develop your awareness of pingala nadi.
Move your consciousness up slowly and evenly through each of the chakras in turn along this curving pathway.
Do not try to synchronize this movement with the breath; simply fix the pingala route firmly in your mind.
Make sure that you are moving in the correct direction from right to left and from left to right.
Forget about everything else and concentrate your total awareness here.
If you make a mistake, go back to mooladhara and start again.
Pingala nadi leaves mooladhara from the right and curves up to swadhisthana, curves to the left crossing manipura, curves to the right crossing anahata, curves to the left crossing vishuddhi, curves to the right and comes to ajna.
The descending passage leaves ajna from the right and curves down to vishuddhi, curves to the left crossing anahata, curves to the right crossing manipura, curves to the left crossing swadhisthana, curves to the right coming to mooladhara.
Continue practising pingala awareness.

Stage 3: Experiencing prana in pingala nadi

Get ready to experience the flow of prana along this passage.

See curving streaks of light as you move your awareness up through pingala.

Try to feel or experience the movement of prana.

Visualize this movement in the form of streaks of light.

If you find it difficult to become aware of the pranic flow at this stage, simply visualize pingala nadi as a slender pathway of light.

When you get used to the flow of consciousness along pingala, then again try to experience the actual pranic movement: first imagination, then move your awareness along the route, then feel the actual movement, the actual sensation of prana and see it as a flowing wave or streak of light.

At first it may be mostly imagination used to see or feel the prana moving along this route.

Do not become discouraged if you do not succeed in the beginning; it takes a great deal of practice.

Stage 4: Introducing the breath

Once you are familiar with the pathway of pingala, you can begin to synchronize the breath with your ascending and descending awareness.

With the inhalation, the breath ascends from the right side of mooladhara and curves into swadhisthana. It leaves swadhisthana from the left and curves into manipura, leaves manipura from the right and curves into anahata, leaves anahata from the left and curves into vishuddhi, leaves vishuddhi from the right, and enters ajna from the right.

With the exhalation, the breath descends from ajna from the right, from vishuddhi to the left, from anahata to the right, from manipura to the left and from swadhisthana to the right, terminating at mooladhara.

Continue the practice.

Direct the consciousness and prana up and down pingala nadi with the movement of the breath.

Observe the gentle, even swing of consciousness as it moves along pingala nadi, through the chakras; be aware of the pranic movement and also be aware of the breath.

If you feel any difficulty doing the practice, repeat the name of each chakra mentally as you pass through it. Ascending: mooladhara right, swadhisthana left, manipura right, anahata left, vishuddhi right, to ajna. Descending: ajna right, vishuddhi left, anahata right, manipura left, swadhisthana right, to mooladhara.

Continue until the process becomes smooth and spontaneous; you should not have to think about it.

Stage 5: Ending the practice

Slowly withdraw your awareness from pingala nadi.

Become aware of your surroundings and all the sounds around you.

Become aware of the room you are in and the people and things within it.

Slowly move your fingers and toes, your hands and feet, gently move your head from side to side.

Take a deep breath and stretch your arms over your head.

Feel the stretch right through the body.

Feel yourself firmly back in your body.

When you have recovered the sensation of your whole physical body, slowly sit up and open your eyes.

Hari Om Tat Sat

PRACTICE 5: CIRCULATING PRANA IN IDA AND PINGALA

Stage 1: Preparation

Take your position, either sitting or lying in shavasana.

If you are lying in shavasana your feet should be about 30 cm apart, your arms should be 5 to 10 cm away from your body with the palms facing up and your head, neck and spine should be in a straight line with the eyes and mouth gently closed.

Begin to surrender the whole body to the floor.

Relax yourself completely as you feel yourself sink down further into the floor with each breath.

If you are sitting up, ensure that the pose you have taken will be comfortable for the duration of the practice.

Place your hands on the knees, in a mudra of your choice.

Balance your body weight on each side equally.

Take your awareness down through your body making yourself completely free from any type of tension or tightness.

Stage 2: Inner space

Begin to observe the whole body mentally; develop total awareness of the body.

Be aware of your physical state and try to attune yourself with your body so that during the practice you will not be distracted by any feeling of discomfort, tension or tightness.

Focus your whole attention at the eyebrow centre.

In front of your closed eyes observe the space called *chidakasha*, the space of *chitta*, consciousness.

Now become aware of *sthulakasha*, the space that fills the entire body.

Be totally aware of the space that pervades the whole body.

In the practice of prana vidya, it is important to develop awareness of the physical space contained within the body.

Direct your consciousness to the inner void and intensify the experience.

Stage 3: Chakra location

Within the space of the body become aware of the spinal passage.

Visualize the chakras shining like bright diamonds or points of light at their locations along the spinal cord.

Begin with the first source of energy, the mooladhara chakra, at the base of the spinal passage.

Visualize the second point of light, swadhisthana chakra, at the coccyx at the lower tip of the spinal cord.

Then be aware of the third centre of prana, the light of manipura chakra, behind the navel in the spinal passage.

Anahata chakra is the fourth point of light energy, situated behind the chest cavity.

Then come up to the fifth point of light in the neck behind the throat pit, vishuddhi chakra.

Finally, see a bright jewel of light in the mid-brain at the top of the spinal cord, ajna chakra.

Visualize all these energy centres in one glance in their proper locations along the spinal passage like beautiful, sparkling, precious stones, strung on a pure silver thread.

Stage 4: Ida and pingala nadis

Once you have developed an awareness of the chakras in the spinal passage, become aware of ida and pingala nadis crisscrossing each other at every chakra point, starting from mooladhara below the spine and coming up to ajna at the top of the spine.

Pingala is the conductor of solar or vital energy, and ida is the conductor of lunar or mental energy.

Focus your awareness at mooladhara chakra, the starting point of these two nadis.

From mooladhara, pingala curves to the right and ida curves to the left; they cross over at each chakra and terminate at ajna.

Develop your inner vision of the chakras and nadis.
Intensify this awareness, even if the experience is based on imagination.
Be aware of the body space and of the spinal passage within this space.
Be aware of the chakras within the spinal passage and the nadis.
Take your awareness once more down to mooladhara chakra and become aware of pingala nadi only.
From mooladhara, pingala curves to the right and crosses through swadhisthana; from swadhisthana it curves to the left and crosses through manipura; from manipura it curves to the right and crosses through anahata; from anahata it curves to the left and crosses through vishuddhi; from vishuddhi it curves to the right and terminates at ajna.
Reverse your awareness back down pingala nadi.
From ajna, pingala curves to the right and crosses through vishuddhi; from vishuddhi it curves to the left and crosses through anahata; from anahata it curves to the right and crosses through manipura; from manipura it curves to the left and crosses through swadhisthana; from swadhisthana it curves to the right and comes back to mooladhara.
Go on for some time circulating the awareness through pingala nadi until the psychic passageway becomes clear.
Now leave awareness of pingala and become aware of ida nadi, starting from mooladhara and moving upward.
From mooladhara, ida curves to the left and crosses through swadhisthana; from swadhisthana it curves to the right and crosses through manipura; from manipura it curves to the left and crosses through anahata; from anahata it curves to the right and crosses through vishuddhi; from vishuddhi it curves to the left and terminates at ajna.
Reverse your awareness to move back down ida nadi.
From ajna chakra, ida curves to the left and crosses through vishuddhi; from vishuddhi it curves to the

right and crosses through anahata; from anahata it curves to the left and crosses through manipura; from manipura it curves to the right and crosses through swadhisthana; then it curves to the left returning to mooladhara.

Continue circulating the awareness through ida nadi for some time.

Once you have developed a clear awareness of ida nadi, cease this practice.

Simply maintain awareness of the chakra locations in the space within the body and of the nadis emanating from mooladhara and crossing over at each chakra.

Stage 5: Introducing the breath and pranic awareness

Now we will introduce breath awareness and awareness of pranic movement.

With the aid of the inhalation, direct your consciousness up pingala nadi from mooladhara to swadhisthana.

With exhalation, bring the awareness back down from swadhisthana to mooladhara through ida nadi.

Add awareness of prana.

During inhalation, be aware of the breath and at the same time be aware of the prana moving through pingala from mooladhara to swadhisthana, then during the exhalation they descend through ida from swadhisthana to mooladhara.

Continue this practice, just moving the awareness, breath and prana between mooladhara and swadhisthana.

Continue for some time and once that practice is established, move on to the next.

Next, with the inhalation raise the awareness up following the path of pingala: from mooladhara, curve to the right and cross swadhisthana, then curve to the left and come to manipura.

During exhalation, follow the path of ida back down to mooladhara: from manipura, leave from the right, curve and enter swadhistana from the right, curve and re-enter mooladhara from the left.

With each inhalation your awareness travels up through pingala to manipura, and with each exhalation it descends to mooladhara through ida nadi.
Intensify your awareness of this process.
Once that is established, practise from mooladhara to anahata.
Consciousness, breath and prana travel together through pingala up to anahata and then descend from anahata to mooladhara via ida.
Intensify this awareness more and more with every breath.
Raise the awareness further up now, from mooladhara to vishuddhi through pingala and descend from vishuddhi to mooladhara through ida.
Ascend with inhalation, being aware of the movement of your awareness.
Descend with the exhalation with equal awareness.
Remain alert. No sleeping.
Now, ascend from mooladhara to ajna through pingala, and descend from ajna to mooladhara through ida.
Each time you reach ajna, maintain the awareness and breath there for a couple of seconds.
Then, with the next exhalation, follow ida back down to mooladhara.
With each inhalation, your awareness travels up through pingala nadi to ajna where you hold it for a few seconds.
Then, with each exhalation, the awareness descends to mooladhara through ida nadi.
Intensify your awareness of this process.
Continue in this way for some time.

Stage 6: Ending the practice

Now leave the awareness of the nadis and chakras and return to breath awareness.
Become aware of the space both within the body and outside the body.
Take your awareness to your natural breathing process.
Become aware of the external environment and all the sounds around you.

Be aware of the position of your body.
Externalize your awareness completely and check that all the senses are giving sensory information about the sounds, smells, tastes in the mouth and feeling of touch.
Slowly and gently move the toes, move the feet, the legs, the fingers, the hands, the arms and the head from side to side.
Take a deep breath in and stretch the whole body.
Then, only when you have regained full awareness of your physical body, gently sit up and open your eyes.

Hari Om Tat Sat

12

Raising and Storing Prana

Practice 1: Mooladhara to manipura rotation
Practice 2: Manipura to ajna rotation
Practice 3: Mooladhara to ajna (via pingala nadi)
Practice 4: Mooladhara to ajna (via sushumna nadi)

In this chapter, the ability to direct prana is explored and developed further. Prana is awakened from mooladhara and consciously raised to ajna where it is stored. During this process prana moves only in one direction, upwards. This occurs on inhalation. On exhalation only the breath and awareness travel back down to mooladhara leaving the prana at ajna. It is at this stage of prana vidya that ajna becomes the focal point of the practice, and in the subsequent stage, the control centre for the distribution of prana.

Initially, the conscious and controlled upward movement of prana occurs through pingala nadi with the normal breath. After some time, ujjayi pranayama and khechari mudra are incorporated to strengthen the practice. Please note that it may take some time before khechari mudra can be practised comfortably for the duration of the practice, especially in a lying position.

Practice 1 and 2 utilize the pingala nadi in two stages: firstly as a rotation from mooladhara to manipura, and secondly as a rotation from manipura to ajna. The rotation of pingala nadi has been divided in this way for learning purposes only. In Practice 3, the skills of Practice 1 and 2 are combined and with the help of ujjayi pranayama and the sustained focus of attention, one begins to raise the energy from mooladhara to ajna through pingala nadi. This requires intense concentration and will take time to perfect. Practice 4 utilizes sushumna nadi.

At the end of each practice, the prana which has been accumulated in ajna must be returned and withdrawn back down to mooladhara. Withdrawal of prana is an important stage of prana vidya as it returns both the energy and the consciousness to its normal state. It must be performed with the same intensity of awareness and attention as the initial stage of the practice.

After the prana has been withdrawn to mooladhara, it is important to check that all the faculties of perception are functioning normally and are under conscious control. The body should be lighter, the senses intact and the understanding present. The practitioner must be aware of the position of the body and the fact that the body is about to be moved. In this way, for a few minutes, the awareness and the senses should be checked systematically. When this has been done, then and only then, has one concluded the practice of prana vidya.

Sometimes it is found that only some of the faculties are present. For example, the sense of sight does not include the faculty of understanding, or there is an awareness of sight and sound but no awareness of time. The solution to this problem is very simple: repeat the last part of the technique. Practise a few rounds of withdrawing the prana from ajna back down to mooladhara. After some time, the eyes can be opened and operating faculties rechecked for their return to normal consciousness.

This problem is rarely faced by beginners and occurs more in advanced stages of the practice. For this reason, the practitioner should move from stage to stage in the recommended sequence. No attempt should be made to miss a stage or hurry through a sequence. Consolidate each stage progressively. The practice of prana vidya should proceed from the elementary stages under the guidance of a qualified person, so that the vision of prana is experienced and the risk of disorientation minimized.

PRACTICE 1: MOOLADHARA TO MANIPURA ROTATION

Stage 1: Preparation

When you have made yourself comfortable and still in your chosen position, make the body and mind calm and peaceful.

If you are sitting up, make sure your body weight is equally distributed on each side.

Begin to observe your breathing process.

As you breathe in and out, totally relax the body.

You are perfectly motionless.

Tell yourself mentally: "I shall not move throughout the duration of the practice. I shall remain aware and alert."

Go inside the body and begin to develop unified awareness of the whole body space as if you are totally empty of anything but air – nothing inside but weightless air – the only physical part of you is the organ of touch, the skin, otherwise you are hollow like a balloon.

Intensify this feeling of inner space.

Stage 2: Chakra and nadi visualization

Begin to visualize the psychic passage, sushumna nadi, as a thin, transparent or white thread running straight up from mooladhara to ajna along the path of the spine.

See this passage clearly and notice the bright chakra jewels or points of light strung along it.

Focus on the first source of light energy, mooladhara chakra, at the base of sushumna.

See it glow and experience a slight throbbing sensation at this point.

Move your awareness up and see swadhisthana chakra, the second point of light, at the tip of the coccyx.

Make it brighter with your imagination and feel it pulsating gently.

Become aware of the third point of light, manipura chakra, behind the navel in sushumna nadi.
Feel a slight pulsation at manipura, and with each pulsation, the point of light or jewel glows more brightly.
Finally, visualize these three chakras: mooladhara, swadhisthana and manipura, all together and make this vision sharp.
Become aware of ida and pingala nadis.
See their curves of light criss-crossing each other at each chakra point.
From mooladhara, pingala curves to the right and ida to the left. They cross each other at swadhisthana, then pingala curves to the left and ida to the right, crossing again at manipura.
Between mooladhara, swadhisthana and manipura, visualize the luminous figure eight created by ida and pingala as they curve between the first three chakras.

Stage 3: Rotation of prana

When you have a clear vision of the figure eight, take your awareness to mooladhara and let it flow with the prana as it follows pingala nadi.
This stream of electric blue-white light leaves mooladhara and enters swadhisthana from the right, then leaves swadhisthana and enters manipura from the left.
Move the awareness and begin the descent through ida nadi. It leaves manipura and enters swadhisthana from the right, then leaves swadhisthana and enters mooladhara from the left.
Trace this pathway with care and attention.
Continue this practice for some time until your awareness travels in an unbroken flow up and down the figure eight.

Stage 4: Breath awareness

When you have accomplished this, begin to synchronize the smooth, curving movement of your awareness with the breath.

Become aware of prana and awareness ascending on the inhalation through pingala nadi in a stream of light from mooladhara to manipura.

The breath and prana should reach manipura at exactly the same time.

Then the prana descends through ida on the exhalation as if it is riding on the breath to mooladhara.

The breath and prana should reach mooladhara at exactly the same time.

Be very alert and aware.

Go on synchronizing the movement of prana with the breath.

Stage 5: Ending the practice

Cease this practice and become aware of the external sounds.

Mentally reconstruct the environment around you.

Focus on your breathing for a few minutes and come back fully into your physical body.

Check to be sure the senses are operating and be aware of the external world. Gradually begin to move the body and open your eyes.

Hari Om Tat Sat

PRACTICE 2: MANIPURA TO AJNA ROTATION

Stage 1: Preparation

Come into a comfortable position for the practice.

You may sit or lie down.

Most importantly, the body should be comfortable, at ease and motionless for the duration of the practice.

As the body settles into the chosen posture check the alignment of the body.

Make sure the weight of the body is evenly distributed on both sides of the body.

Be aware of the head, neck and spine forming the midline of the body, and the right and left side mirror each other.

Body perfectly aligned and balanced, relaxed and at ease.

Be aware of the developing stillness and space within the body.

Focus for a few moments on the inner space within the body and allow the feeling to intensify.

Stage 2: Chakra location

Become aware of the psychic spinal passage, the sushumna nadi, and the chakras strung along its length like points of light or sparkling jewels.

The first is mooladhara chakra, the second, swadhisthana chakra and the third is manipura chakra.

Focus on manipura chakra, the point of light related to the solar plexus.

Above it is anahata chakra, the fourth point of light in sushumna nadi, behind the sternum on the inner wall of the spinal column.

Focus on this point of light at anahata.

In the cervical plexus behind the throat pit is vishuddhi chakra, the fifth point of light.

Focus on this radiant spot.

At the top of the spinal cord in the mid-brain, directly behind the eyebrow centre is ajna chakra, the sixth point of light.

Focus your awareness at this point.

Intensify your awareness of manipura, anahata, vishuddhi and ajna chakras so that you can see all four at one single glance.

See them all glowing and throbbing brightly.

Stage 3: Ida and pingala visualization

Become aware of the luminous pathways of ida and pingala criss-crossing at each chakra point.

From manipura pingala curves to the right and ida to the left.

They cross at anahata then pingala curves to the left and ida to the right.

They cross at vishuddhi then pingala curves to and enters ajna from the right, while ida curves to and enters ajna from the left.

Between the four points of bright light visualize the three interlacing curves of ida and pingala nadis.

Stage 4: Rotation of prana

When this vision is completely clear, take your awareness to manipura and begin to ascend, following pingala nadi with your awareness.

This stream of brilliant light leaves manipura and enters anahata from the right.

Then it leaves anahata and enters vishuddhi from the left.

From vishuddhi it curves towards and enters ajna from the right.

Begin descending with the prana through ida nadi.

Ida leaves ajna from the left and enters vishuddhi from the left.

It then leaves vishuddhi and enters anahata from the right.

From anahata it curves towards and enters manipura from the left.

Combine the practice so that you are ascending from manipura to ajna through pingala, and descending from ajna to manipura through ida.

Go on tracing this pathway with care and attention.

Stage 5: Breath awareness

When you can do this successfully, begin to synchronize the movement of prana and awareness with the breath.

As you breathe in, ascend from manipura through pingala nadi to ajna, feeling or visualizing the stream of prana which reaches ajna at the same time as the breath.

Then the prana descends with the breath, curving down through ida nadi to manipura.

The end of the exhalation and the prana should reach manipura at the same time.

Go on rotating the awareness through the passages, synchronizing the movement of prana with the breath.

Stage 6: Ending the practice

On the next exhalation, release awareness of the nadis and the vision of prana.

Focus the attention on the breath.

Notice the sound of the breath, the sensation of the breath in the nostrils, in the chest and in the abdomen.

Feel the breath contained within the body structure.

Deepen the breath slightly and experience the physical body.

Be aware of the posture, the placement of limbs, head, neck and trunk.

Feel the weight of the body.

Now recall the room; visualize it in as much detail as possible.

Mentally see yourself within the room.

Be aware of sounds in the external environment.

Allow these sounds to externalize the awareness completely.

Prepare to move the body.

The practice is now complete.

Hari Om Tat Sat

PRACTICE 3: MOOLADHARA TO AJNA (VIA PINGALA NADI)

Stage 1: Preparation

Prepare for the practice.

Choose a comfortable posture that you can maintain for the whole practice.

Ideally the body remains still and steady throughout.

Settle the body, make any adjustments and then cease all movement.

Relax physically and mentally and allow stillness to develop.

Be aware of the whole body structure, its shape and form.

Internalize the awareness and be aware of the inner space, the space within the whole body.

Commence ujjayi and khechari mudra, and become conscious of sensations within the inner space.

Continue for some time.

Stage 2: Awakening prana in pingala nadi

Now you are going to awaken prana in pingala nadi, which starts from mooladhara.

From mooladhara it goes out to the right.

Then it curves back to cross through swadhisthana.

Then with a curve to the left it comes to manipura.

With a curve to the right it comes to anahata.

With a curve to the left it meets vishuddhi.

And with a curve to the right it joins ajna chakra.

From ajna, bring your consciousness straight down to mooladhara via sushumna.

On inhalation start awakening your prana.

Use ujjayi pranayama; take long deep breaths and feel the ujjayi breath drawing the prana up to ajna.

Utilizing ujjayi pranayama, inhale – mooladhara, swadhisthana, manipura, anahata, vishuddhi, ajna.

Exhale – go straight down to mooladhara via sushumna on your ujjayi exhalation.

However, although prana travels up to ajna during inhalation, only the awareness, not the prana, travels back down to mooladhara during exhalation.

The energy travels up but only the awareness travels down.

Each time you reach ajna, maintain the awareness there for a couple of seconds as you hold the breath, and be aware of the increasing pranic energy held at ajna as bright light.

Go on experiencing the streaks of light shooting up to accumulate at ajna bringing only the awareness back through sushumna.

Practise a maximum of 49 rounds.

Stage 3: Returning prana to mooladhara

You have collected the prana at ajna in the form of light energy.

In order to maintain your energy balance once the practice is over, the prana must be properly returned to its original source at mooladhara.

Using your powers of concentration and synchronizing the movement with the breath, focus your attention at ajna and flow down sushumna nadi with your ujjayi exhalation, carrying the prana back to its source at mooladhara.

At mooladhara, hold the breath for a few moments as you deposit the prana, then simply raise your awareness to ajna as you inhale without carrying any prana.

With each breath you are returning prana to mooladhara.

Remain alert and continue the practice with full concentration until you are sure you have returned all the energy to its source.

Stage 4: Ending the practice

Stop the ujjayi breathing and be aware of the normal breath.

Be aware of the taste in the mouth, any scent you can pick up as you breathe in and out.

Notice the contact points between the body and the floor.

Slowly and carefully begin to externalize your awareness, become aware of your surroundings, recall the time of day.

Become aware of the outside sounds.
Mentally reconstruct the environment around you.
Focus on your breathing for a few minutes and come back fully into your physical body.
Gradually begin to move the body; slowly open your eyes.
If, however, upon opening your eyes you find that you are not fully back in your physical body and returned to your normal state of functioning awareness, it means that you have not completely withdrawn the prana from ajna chakra.
So, again close the eyes and with the ujjayi breath repeat, calmly and steadily, three more rounds of carrying the prana back down from ajna to mooladhara.
Then, once more, slowly externalize your awareness in the prescribed manner.
If you wish, practise palming and then gently open the eyes.

Hari Om Tat Sat

PRACTICE 4: MOOLADHARA TO AJNA (VIA SUSHUMNA NADI)

Stage 1: Preparation

Assume a comfortable pose and make sure the spine and head are in a straight line.

The eyes and mouth should be gently closed.

Become aware of the body and of the position of the whole body as one unit; feel the body as one unit.

Feel the body gradually becoming still.

Concentrate on motionlessness.

Complete awareness of the body and the stillness that you feel within the body.

Stage 2: Chakra awareness

Become aware of the spinal cord.

Take your awareness to the perineum, just below the spinal cord, and become aware of mooladhara chakra.

Mentally repeat 'mooladhara'.

Move up to the coccyx at the tip of the spinal cord and locate swadhisthana.

Mentally repeat 'swadhisthana'.

Now shift your awareness further up the spine to the point directly behind the navel and mentally repeat 'manipura'.

Next, come up the spine to the point behind the heart.

Experience the location of anahata and mentally repeat 'anahata'.

Take your awareness up the spine again, to the neck.

Become aware of the location of vishuddhi directly behind the throat pit and mentally repeat 'vishuddhi'.

Move your awareness up to the top of the spine at the mid-brain, directly behind the eyebrow centre.

Locate ajna there and mentally repeat 'ajna'.

Finally, come up to the crown of the head.

Experience sahasrara and mentally repeat 'sahasrara'.

Reverse the direction of your awareness and come down again through the chakras repeating their names mentally as you locate them one by one.

Continue moving up and down the spine repeating the chakra names until you are able to locate each chakra point effortlessly.

Then become aware of all the chakras together in one inner glance.

Visualize all the chakra points together in their proper locations like tiny, bright lights, sparkling diamonds or red rubies strung on a silver thread.

Stage 3: Visualizing prana in sushumna nadi

Now visualize the psychic passage in the spine from mooladhara all the way up to ajna.

See all the chakra points connected by sushumna nadi which flows straight up piercing the centre of each chakra.

Intensify the awareness of this passage within the spinal cord extending from mooladhara to ajna.

We are going to awaken the prana.

Remember that prana is always visualized in the form of light streaks or particles of light moving at great speed.

To gain the experience of the existence of prana, first become aware of the ascent and descent of pranic energy in sushumna.

Experience the movement of prana from its nucleus in mooladhara chakra to its distribution centre at ajna.

Experience prana not in the form of a picture, but as an actual feeling of energy movement within the body.

With practice, the feeling of prana flowing in the straight pranic passage, sushumna, along the spine from mooladhara to ajna chakra becomes totally clear.

Stage 4: Storing prana at ajna

When the experience of sushumna nadi is clear, inhale with the normal breath and direct the awareness of prana up the passage from mooladhara to ajna chakra.

Focus the awareness at ajna and retain the breath there for two seconds while storing the prana.

Then, exhale back down the passage from ajna to mooladhara leaving the prana at ajna.

You do not have to repeat the names of the chakras; just be aware of their locations as you pass through them.
Again while inhaling, experience the pranic force moving up along sushumna from mooladhara to ajna.
Focus the awareness at ajna as you retain the breath for two seconds.
At the end of each ascent of consciousness and prana with the breath, there is a momentary *kumbhaka*, retention, at ajna; the breathing is not a continuous process.
After ascending with inhalation retain the breath for two seconds at ajna before exhalation.
With exhalation, bring the awareness back down to mooladhara.
Continue with this practice, focusing the awareness and the prana at ajna as you retain the breath for two seconds, then exhaling back down to mooladhara.
With each inhalation, be aware of the prana moving up from mooladhara to ajna.
With each exhalation, be aware of the breath going down from ajna to mooladhara.
In between inhalation and exhalation there is a short break, a retention of breath for two seconds at ajna.
During this time focus your awareness on the prana at ajna chakra.
Intensify your awareness of the movement of prana along sushumna.
Do not sleep or allow the mind to wander.
Awareness and prana move up the psychic passage during inhalation and awareness moves down during exhalation.
The movement of prana should be intensely felt flowing up sushumna nadi.
This practice involves moving the awareness.
Move the awareness to actually create the feeling of prana moving along the pranic passage, then relax as the awareness moves down on exhalation.

With each inhalation, intensify the awareness of prana coming up from mooladhara to ajna, its form is a stream of white light ascending along sushumna.

At the end of inhalation retain the breath and prana for two seconds with your full attention focused at the eyebrow centre, at ajna chakra, and feel the energy building there.

Then exhale down sushumna, moving just the awareness from ajna to mooladhara.

This can be practised 27 times.

Stage 5: Returning prana to mooladhara

Now you will move the prana back down from ajna chakra, where it has been stored, to mooladhara chakra.

Focus your full awareness at ajna chakra; be aware of the pranic energy you have stored there.

Visualize this dynamic force in the form of a dazzlingly bright, white light.

Be aware of any sensations of heat or throbbing you may experience at ajna.

Then, slowly and carefully, begin to direct the prana straight back down through sushumna to mooladhara with the exhalation.

Visualize the descent of the white stream of light moving down sushumna.

It is of vital importance that all the prana is brought back down, so go on systematically with this return of the prana to mooladhara until you are quite sure none remains at ajna.

Stage 6: Ending the practice

When you feel sure all the prana has been returned, leave awareness of the chakras and nadis and become aware of the breath.

Gently come back to awareness of annamaya kosha, the gross physical body.

Be aware of all the distant and nearby sounds around; mentally reconstruct the environment around you.

Check that all the senses are functioning properly.

Be aware of the taste in the mouth, move the tongue a little, and the lips.

Focus your attention on your breath for a few moments and be aware of the sense of smell.

If you feel a little vague or not properly grounded in the senses and physical body, practise a few more rounds, descending the prana in sushumna.

Check that you are fully back in your physical body, then slowly begin to move the body, practise palming and open your eyes.

Hari Om Tat Sat

Practice note: In the beginning, the practitioner should do no more than 27 rounds. Over some time the rounds can be increased until a maximum of 49 rounds is completed. However, when the awakening sensation of prana is distinctly felt, counting up to 49 rounds is no longer necessary. Once an actual experience of the awakening of prana has commenced and movements of the pranic force from mooladhara to ajna are clearly felt, one can then journey further into prana vidya, expanding and distributing the prana for healing purposes.

13

Expansion, Relaxation and Contraction of Prana

INTRODUCING EXPANSION WITH UJJAYI

Practice 1: Expansion and relaxation
Practice 2: Expansion and contraction

AWAKENING AND EXPANDING PRANA

Practice 3: Expansion and relaxation (with chakra awareness)
Practice 4: Expansion and contraction (with pancha prana awareness)

This chapter introduces, first, the practice of 'expansion and relaxation', and second, 'expansion and contraction' of the pranic body. Both practices utilize ujjayi pranayama or psychic breath, which facilitates a subtle and psychic experience. As a result of the force of ujjayi pranayama, the pranic body is expanded on inhalation and either relaxed or contracted on exhalation. Although ujjayi is being performed, the awareness must become totally absorbed in the experience of expansion and relaxation or expansion and contraction. The entire consciousness, the entire faculty of imagination becomes focused on expansion and relaxation or contraction while the process of ujjayi breathing continues in the background.

Some practitioners may experience difficulty drawing the awareness away from the ujjayi breathing process. In this case, one should become aware of how, in japa or ajapa, one's awareness shifts from the breath to the mantra. The concept is the same, that is, inhalation and exhalation continue but the awareness is with the expansion and relaxation or contraction of the pranic body. Gradually the awareness is shifted away from the breath until psychic expansion and contraction or relaxation is experienced exclusively.

In the more advanced practice, the pores of the body become the mechanism for breathing. This ujjayi breath becomes all-pervading. Initially, the imagination may be used; however, as one enters deeper into the practice one becomes aware that every pore of the body is breathing energy in and out. On inhalation, energy is breathed in through every pore of the body, which expands like a balloon. On exhalation, the energy is rapidly breathed out through every pore and the body becomes as light as cotton. Throughout the practice of prana vidya, ujjayi is the basic breathing technique utilized.

Start with 27 rounds and gradually build up to 49. The recommended length for each session is no more than 49 rounds. Each stage of the practice is to be continued patiently and the techniques mastered and the experience stabilized before moving on to distributing prana.

INTRODUCING EXPANSION WITH UJJAYI

PRACTICE 1: EXPANSION AND RELAXATION

Stage 1: Preparation

Sit in a comfortable asana and place the hands in chin or jnana mudra.

Practise kaya sthairyam for a few minutes, developing stillness and steadiness within the physical body.

Stage 2: Commencing ujjayi pranayama

Commence ujjayi pranayama, the psychic breath, and allow the awareness to become subtler.

Follow the sound and rhythm of the ujjayi breath while becoming increasingly more sensitive to pranamaya kosha, the pranic body.

Continue to follow ujjayi until only the breath and sensations of the subtle body pervade the awareness.

Stage 3: Expansion and relaxation

Prepare now to expand the pranic body.

With each inhalation, the body expands as if it is breathing in through every pore.

With each exhalation, the body relaxes as if it is breathing out through every pore.

Continue to practise ujjayi pranayama and feel the energy being pulled in through every pore on each inhalation; expand while inhaling, and relax while exhaling.

Here ujjayi is not following the path of a nadi as in most of the other practices; it is pervading throughout the body. When you inhale utilizing ujjayi, every pore inhales prana and the body expands.

When your body exhales utilizing ujjayi, prana is released from every pore and the body relaxes.

Synchronize your body consciousness with breath awareness and the movement of prana.

Now, as you inhale, visualize streaks of dazzling, blue-white light flashing through your body in all directions; they move at lightning speed.

See your whole body charged with countless shooting sparks.

Then, as you relax the body with exhalation, visualize the movement of these light streaks slowing down or diminishing in brightness.

This is all done in coordination with ujjayi pranayama.

Inhale and expand.

Exhale and relax.

Keep on practising.

Now you should get so used to ujjayi that it goes on automatically, while your entire consciousness and the faculty of awareness are centred on the feeling of expansion and relaxation.

Become indifferent to the breathing process.

The entire consciousness should follow the forces of prana that are expanding and relaxing the astral or pranic body.

Your total awareness should be absorbed in expansion and relaxation, not the breath, although ujjayi breathing continues in the background.

Count up to 49 rounds in this way.

Stage 4: Ending the practice

Prepare now to end the practice.

Release the experience of expansion and relaxation.

Let go of the ujjayi breath and be aware of the inner space.

Gradually deepen the breath and feel once more the structure of the physical body.

Experience the solidity and weight of the body, and feel the support of the ground or chair beneath the body.

Externalize the awareness further, recall the room and mentally visualize all the details within the room.

Notice sounds within or outside the room, sounds both near and far.

Recall the time of day and know that you have been practising expansion and relaxation of the pranic body.

The practice is now complete.

Bring the awareness back to the physical body and prepare to move the body.

Make small movements to begin with and when you are ready, when you feel completely externalized, gently open the eyes.

Hari Om Tat Sat

Practice note: The next practice is similar to Practice 1 except that during exhalation there will be a contraction of the pranic body instead of relaxation. When the consciousness and pranas are withdrawn from the whole body and directed back to ajna and held there, the body contracts. This contraction is a *bandha*, or psychic lock. It can be likened to a mental moolabandha experienced throughout the entire body. If both the concept and the visualization are clear, the whole body will expand and contract psychically. If you cannot do this yet, you need more practice in the earlier techniques of prana vidya.

PRACTICE 2: EXPANSION AND CONTRACTION

Stage 1: Preparation

Come into a comfortable position of your choice.

Take time to adjust the body so it can remain still throughout the practice.

When the body is at ease, allow it to become still.

For a few moments, maintain awareness of the physical body and intensify the quality of stillness.

Shift the awareness to the breathing process.

Observe each and every breath moving within the body.

The rhythm of the breath is natural and spontaneous.

Stage 2: Commencing ujjayi pranayama

Gradually introduce the ujjayi breath and place the tongue in khechari mudra.

Focus your full awareness on the soft, deep ujjayi breathing in the throat.

Be totally attentive to this rhythmic flow for some time; it is so subtle that you can hardly hear it.

Stage 3: Expansion and contraction

Prepare now to expand and contract the pranic body.

Inhale utilizing the ujjayi breath and draw the prana in through the entire body.

Prana is drawn in through the pores and the energy expands.

Exhale utilizing ujjayi and release the prana from every part of the body.

Let the prana move out through the pores, and feel the pranic body contract.

On inhalation, mentally feel the energy expanding in all directions.
It is not physical expansion but psychic expansion.
The whole body from head to toe is saturated with pranic energy; feel this intensely.
Simultaneously, your psychic body is expanding in all directions.
When you exhale, relax and then consciously withdraw your prana from all parts of the body.
Just as the water of the ocean recedes when the tide flows out, so also the prana recedes during exhalation, and contraction takes place.
The body as one homogeneous unit is expanded and contracted.
Inhale and expand.
Exhale, relax and contract.
Continue for some time, but do not exceed 49 rounds.

Stage 4: Ending the practice

Prepare now to end the practice.
Release expansion and contraction.
Let go of the ujjayi breath and khechari mudra.
Become aware of the natural breath moving effortlessly within the physical body.
Be aware of the movement of the inhalation and exhalation in the body.
Experience the physical body in the chosen posture, its shape and form.
Gradually become aware of the external environment, of the room in which you are sitting, of the external sounds.
Check the senses systematically.
Externalize your awareness completely and make sure you are grounded in the physical body.
When you are ready, make small movements and gently open the eyes.
The practice is now complete.

Hari Om Tat Sat

PRACTICE 3: EXPANSION AND RELAXATION (WITH CHAKRA AWARENESS)

Stage 1: Preparation

Assume a comfortable posture and relax the body making sure it is free of tension.

Become aware of the breath.

Commence ujjayi breathing and place the tongue in khechari mudra.

Notice any thoughts passing through the mind and let them drop away.

Continue to focus on the sound of ujjayi until the body and mind become still and steady.

Stage 2: Tracing pingala nadi

Take your awareness inside the body and observe the inner space.

Within the space of the body visualize the chakras and the nadis in their respective positions.

Take your awareness to pingala nadi curving along the spine.

Intensify your awareness of the energy flowing in pingala nadi.

Carefully take your awareness up pingala nadi: from mooladhara it curves to the right and crosses through swadhisthana; from swadhisthana it curves to the left and crosses through manipura; from manipura it curves to the right and crosses through anahata; from anahata it curves to the left and crosses through vishuddhi and from vishuddhi it curves to the right and finally enters ajna from the right.

Develop your awareness of pingala nadi.

Now begin to synchronize the ujjayi breath with your awareness of pingala nadi.

As you breathe in, breath and awareness rise from mooladhara to ajna along pingala.

As you breathe out, breath and awareness descend in a straight line down sushumna nadi from ajna to mooladhara.
Synchronize the breath with the ascent and descent of awareness.
Continue for some time, until the circuit becomes natural.

Stage 3: Awakening and raising prana

At this stage, start to awaken the experience of prana.
Visualize a stream of light particles in pingala nadi.
With the inhalation, move the awareness of prana up pingala from mooladhara to ajna chakra.
Deposit the prana at ajna and retain the breath there for a few seconds.
Then exhale and bring the awareness back down to mooladhara through sushumna, leaving the prana stored at ajna.
With total attention and alertness of mind, develop this awareness of the pranic flow from mooladhara to ajna.
There is no distinction between the flow of the inhalation, the movement of prana and your awareness; all are united.
The awareness, the breath and the prana ascend as one force, one power, from mooladhara along pingala nadi up to ajna.
Now, as you pass through each chakra, intensify the awareness by mentally repeating its name once.
As you ascend with the inhalation, say mentally to yourself: 'mooladhara, swadhisthana, manipura, anahata, vishuddhi, ajna'.
At ajna the inhalation should be complete.
Hold the breath at ajna for few seconds while repeating mentally: 'ajna, ajna, ajna, ajna, ajna', five times.
Then exhale and bring the breath and awareness straight down sushumna to mooladhara.
Again, raise the prana with the next inhalation.
Experience the awakening of prana at mooladhara and the raising of this pranic force through pingala nadi.

Only when you have experienced this can you commence your journey further into the practice of prana vidya, so develop this awareness carefully.
Do not sleep.
Be completely alert and aware of the practice, your mind should not wander.
Continue for some time.
With watchful awareness observe the movement of prana from mooladhara to ajna; let your breath and consciousness rise through pingala nadi with the pranic energy.
Hold your awareness and the breath at ajna and intensify the experience of prana.
Experience the prana building up at ajna; see the light at ajna becoming more and more luminous.

Stage 4: Expansion and relaxation

Be totally aware of the rhythmic, even flow of ujjayi breath for some time.
Then, expand your awareness of the breathing process and begin to experience breathing in and out through each and every pore of your body.
As you breathe in, feel that you are drawing in air through the entire surface of the skin.
As you breathe out, feel the air being released through the millions of tiny pores from the top of the head right down to the fingertips and toes.
The whole organ of the skin is breathing as one vitally alive unit.
Imagine that, as you breathe in, your whole body is beginning to gently expand outward like a balloon being pumped up with air.
Then, as you breathe out through all your pores simultaneously, simply let the whole body relax.
Just let go as you breathe out.
Continue watching each breath with close attention and feel your whole body breathing.
Upon inhalation, the space contained within your body expands evenly like a balloon being puffed up with air.

Upon exhalation, your body comes back to its normal size while body and mind relax completely.

Continue with this practice of expansion and relaxation.

Upon inhalation, your whole body is full of streaks of intense light energy.

Upon exhalation, you relax and the movement and brightness of this light energy diminishes and relaxes.

Experience this pranic energy vividly and be aware of the pranic movement throughout the entire body.

Stage 5: Returning prana to mooladhara

Now you are going to return the prana to mooladhara.

Inhale and hold your awareness at ajna; experience the build-up of prana you have stored there. See the glowing, pranic light at ajna.

Then, exhaling, take the prana straight back down through sushumna to mooladhara.

Inhale and take just the awareness to ajna, exhale and direct the awareness and prana back down sushumna to mooladhara.

Continue this practice until you are absolutely sure all the prana has been returned to mooladhara.

Stage 6: Ending the practice

When all the prana is back in mooladhara chakra, leave your awareness of the chakras and nadis.

Let go of the ujjayi breath and khechari mudra.

Become aware of the natural breath moving effortlessly within the physical body.

Become aware of your whole physical body and its position.

Gradually become aware of the external environment, of the room you are in, of the external sounds.

Systematically check the senses to ensure a return to normal functioning.

If necessary, do a few descents from ajna to mooladhara to return all excess prana.

Externalize your awareness completely and make sure you are back in your annamaya kosha, the gross physical body.

Slowly begin to move your limbs and, only when you are fully back in your body, gently open your eyes.

Hari Om Tat Sat

PRACTICE 4: EXPANSION AND CONTRACTION (WITH PANCHA PRANA AWARENESS)

Stage 1: Preparation

When you have made yourself comfortable and still in your chosen position, allow the body and mind to become calm and peaceful.

If you are sitting up, make sure your body weight is equally distributed on each side.

Commence ujjayi pranayama.

As you breathe in and out, totally relax the body.

You are perfectly motionless.

Tell yourself mentally, "I shall not move throughout the duration of the practice. I shall remain aware and alert."

Go inside the body and begin to develop unified awareness of the whole body space as if you are totally empty of anything but air and an outer shell.

Nothing inside but weightless air; the only physical part of you is the organ of skin, otherwise you are hollow like a balloon.

Intensify this feeling of inner space.

Stage 2: Visualizing the five pranas

Visualize or feel vyana, the energy that pervades the whole body in the form of streaks of light.

See these blue-white currents of light darting rapidly throughout each and every part of the body, pervading it entirely from head to toe.

Feel this subtle movement with full awareness.

Next, visualize udana in the legs, arms and head as spirals, rings of light energy or circles of light, moving clockwise toward the outer tips of the extremities.

It spirals from hips to toes, shoulders to fingertips, and throat to the top of the head at great speed.

Have an instant visualization of this continuous, spiralling energy in the extremities of the body.

Then concentrate on samana between the diaphragm and the navel.

Experience it as waves of light travelling from left to right and back again like a fast shuttle on a weaving loom.

The feeling and visualization should be instantaneous.

Leave samana and become aware of apana, the energy moving between the navel and perineum in waves of downward moving light.

Lastly, become aware of prana as waves of upward moving light energy moving between the diaphragm and the throat.

Be aware of the five pranas in their respective locations within the body.

Stage 3: Tracing pingala nadi

Leave awareness of the five pranas.

Visualize the spinal column between mooladhara and ajna chakra.

In the centre of the spinal cord, see the transparent or silvery-white psychic pathway.

See the chakra points strung along it like brightly shining jewels on a thread.

Then begin to weave the luminous pingala pathway; it leaves mooladhara from the right, curves to the right, crosses through swadhisthana then curves left through manipura. From there it curves right through anahata, next it curves left through vishuddhi and, finally, it curves right and comes to ajna.

From ajna, begin to descend pingala nadi curving right through vishuddhi, left through anahata, right through manipura, left through swadhisthana and, finally, right back to mooladhara where it began.

Move your awareness slowly and evenly up and down this passage, intensifying pingala awareness.

Now visualize and feel waves or streaks of pranic light spiralling up through pingala.
Actually experience the sensation of prana flowing in this passage.
As you visualize the prana, begin to synchronize the ujjayi breath with ascending and descending awareness.
With inhalation, the prana ascends from mooladhara, crossing swadhisthana, manipura, anahata and vishuddhi, terminating at ajna.
With exhalation, the prana descends from ajna crossing vishuddhi, anahata, manipura, swadhisthana, terminating at mooladhara.
Go on observing the gentle, even swing of breath, prana and consciousness as it spirals along pingala nadi.
The process should now be so familiar to you that you no longer have to think about it.

Stage 4: Raising prana

Perform the practice with absolute concentration, feeling the movement of prana with ever-increasing intensity.
Begin now to raise and store the prana in ajna chakra.
Continue awakening the pranic force and directing it along the pingala psychic passage from mooladhara to ajna.
Each time you inhale and reach ajna, remain there in a short kumbhaka, internal breath retention, while you mentally repeat the name 'ajna' five times.
On exhalation, only the awareness and breath return to mooladhara.
The breathing is gentle, spontaneous ujjayi.
Concentrate on the movement of awareness and prana from mooladhara to ajna along pingala nadi.
The smooth, curving swing of awareness from one chakra to another should come naturally to you.
When you experience a build up of the luminous energy in ajna, leave awareness of the prana moving upward in pingala nadi and focus on the slow, deep ujjayi breathing.
Be aware of the whole body.

Stage 5: Expansion and contraction

Become aware of your body full of light and energy.

Change your concept of the normal breathing process and create the experience of breathing, not through the nose and lungs, rather breathe in and out through every pore in your skin.

The length of your inhalation and exhalation should be equal.

Each pore is breathing in and out independently and in unison with the other pores.

As you breathe in, feel that you are drawing air in through the entire surface of the skin.

As you breathe out, all the millions of tiny pores are simultaneously expelling air.

The whole skin area, from head to toe, is breathing in and out as one unit.

Try to actually feel your pores expanding every time you breathe in.

Experience your skin as a highly dynamic organ.

As you breathe in through all your pores, experience that your whole inner space begins to expand outward from head to toe.

Feel this gentle expanding sensation as if you are a balloon being blown up with air.

Then, as you breathe out through every pore, feel this space within the body contracting slightly.

Intensify this experience of the body expanding upon inhalation and contracting upon exhalation.

Stage 6: Adding pranic awareness

Now become aware of the effect this practice has on the prana which pervades the entire space within the body in the form of light.

As you inhale, visualize this light expanding through the body like lightning streaks; it is whitish-blue or silvery-white in colour and shoots in every direction.

As you exhale, this pranic energy contracts.

Upon inhalation the light body expands, upon exhalation it contracts.

Concentrate your whole attention upon this light field, the pranamaya kosha, expanding and contracting with the breath. Continue until the vision of prana fades.

Stage 7: Returning prana to mooladhara

Now you are going to return the prana to mooladhara.

Return your awareness to ajna; experience the build-up of the prana you stored there previously. See any glowing, pranic light remaining at ajna.

Then, exhaling, take the prana straight back down through sushumna to mooladhara.

Inhale and return just the awareness to ajna, exhale and direct any prana back down sushumna to mooladhara.

Continue this practice until you are absolutely sure all the prana has been returned to mooladhara.

Stage 8: Ending the practice

When all the prana has been returned, shift the awareness to the natural breath.

Observe the breathing process occurring spontaneously within the body.

Gradually become aware of your whole physical body and its position.

Be aware of the breath and the body.

Extend the awareness beyond the body and tune into the external environment.

Recall the room in which you are sitting.

Listen to the sounds around you.

Check the senses systematically; sense of taste, smell, touch and hearing.

Externalize your awareness completely.

Draw the awareness back into the physical body.

When you are ready, slowly begin to move and gently open your eyes.

The practice is now complete.

Hari Om Tat Sat

14

Distribution of Prana

INTERNAL DISTRIBUTION

Practice 1: Expansion and relaxation
Practice 2: Expansion and contraction

EXTERNAL DISTRIBUTION

Practice 3: Expansion and relaxation
Practice 4: Expansion and contraction

VISION OF PRANA SHAKTI

Practice 5: Vision of prana shakti

Distribution of prana involves concentration on and direction of prana. From ajna the prana is directed throughout the body by the process of psychic expansion-relaxation or expansion-contraction. When the prana is distributed from ajna there is expansion, and when it is withdrawn back to ajna there is relaxation or contraction. Internal distribution of prana refers to directing prana within one's own body. Prana is visualized and consciously and wilfully distributed to specific parts of the body as well as to the body as a whole. External distribution refers to extending prana externally to the surrounding environment.

Distribution of prana has no barriers or limitations and may be distributed in all directions.

During distribution, the power of visualization is utilized; prana is visualized as streams of light and directed from ajna to the body and beyond. Before external distribution, a *yantra* or form, such as a triangle, circle or cross is visualized surrounding or passing through the body. It defines the area of the body and acts as a safeguard, supporting the return to 'normal' consciousness at the end of the practice. Once the supporting yantra has been visualized, prana is expanded outwards using the method of expansion and relaxation, or expansion and contraction.

For these practices of distribution of energy, prana is progressively awakened, raised and stored in ajna, distributed internally and/or externally and finally returned to mooladhara, its source. This process has a unique balancing effect on the mind, leading the practitioner through the successive stages of *pratyahara*, sense withdrawal, and *dharana*, concentration. Instead of stopping or stilling the mind by force, these practices raise and balance the energy, which indirectly has a tranquillizing effect on the mind. This enables the practitioner to experience deeper levels of meditation than may be possible through other practices.

Within this chapter is the practice of psychically dissolving or melting the body, part by part, until the pranamaya kosha or pranic body is directly experienced. The practice aims to obtain a vision or direct experience of prana, of pure light. It is possible to practise prana vidya for years and years without having the actual 'vision of prana'. However, unless the practitioner attains this vision, perfection in prana vidya cannot be achieved. Whenever the eyes are closed and the prana sadhana is mentally or psychically tuned into, the vision of light must come spontaneously and effortlessly. Just as darkness comes without effort, the vision of light must come quickly and without effort. It is not included in the preparatory practices as its effect is very powerful and sometimes frightening. For this reason, previous experience and understanding is required before commencing.

INTERNAL DISTRIBUTION

Practice note: Expansion and contraction of the heart is strictly forbidden in prana vidya. It is the only part or organ for which this process is prohibited. Only people who are under the strict guidance of a guru or master of prana vidya can practise expansion and contraction of the heart muscle safely.

PRACTICE 1: EXPANSION AND RELAXATION

Stage 1: Preparation

You may lie down, stand up, sit in a meditation asana or sit on a chair.

Ensure the body is comfortable, make all necessary adjustments.

Once settled in the chosen posture, allow the body to relax and become still, making sure the spine is straight.

Shift the awareness to the natural breath flowing in and out of the body.

Follow the breath for some time, developing stillness and steadiness of body and mind.

Effortlessly and naturally move into ujjayi pranayama and khechari mudra.

Stage 2: Awakening and raising prana

Moving with the inhalation, begin to follow the psychic passage of pingala nadi from mooladhara to ajna.

On the exhalation, the awareness and breath follow the psychic passage of pingala nadi back down from ajna to mooladhara.

Go on for some time circulating the breath and the awareness up and down pingala.

Once established in this practice, visualize prana moving along with the breath and awareness.

Streams of white light moving up and down pingala nadi.

At the end of the next inhalation, pause at ajna to store the awakened prana there. Return only the awareness back down to mooladhara.

Continue in this way until ajna becomes a storehouse of luminous light.

Stage 3: Expansion and relaxation

Move the awareness from ajna to the breath.

Focus on the soft, rhythmic sound of ujjayi.

Simultaneously with the breath, develop awareness of expansion and relaxation.

This movement should not be muscular.

The body should not move at all; it is pranic and psychic expansion.

Be aware of the expansion and relaxation of the pranic body while practising ujjayi pranayama.

With every breath develop the experience of expansion and relaxation.

Stage 4: Distribution

Remain with the experience of expansion and relaxation and prepare to distribute prana to different parts of the body.

On inhalation, prana is directed from ajna to the chosen part of the body, and on the exhalation, relax and withdraw the prana back to ajna.

Start distributing, for example:

Right arm: To begin, supply prana from ajna to the right arm.

With the inhalation, distribute prana to the right arm from ajna.

With the exhalation, relax and withdraw the prana back to ajna chakra.

On inhalation, direct the energy to the right arm; direct the prana in and around the right arm.

On exhalation, relax the right arm.

The centre is ajna; from ajna start the whole process of distribution.

Send prana to the fingertips, hand, forearm, upper arm, to every part of the right arm.

Fill every cell with prana throughout your right arm.

Feel the movement of prana from ajna throughout the right arm.

Withdraw the prana from the right arm and return it back to ajna.

Left arm: Practise the same as was done for the right arm.

Come back to ajna first and retain the breath.

Go to the left arm and fill it with prana out to the fingertips.

Withdraw the prana back to ajna.

Prana proceeds from ajna to the left arm and returns from the left arm back to ajna.

You are only distributing the prana and experiencing the pranic field expanding and relaxing.

Come back to ajna, retain the breath there for a few seconds.

Exhale and relax.

Right leg: With the inhalation, supply prana to your right leg.

If flows from ajna inside the body through the right side of your back and hip into your right leg; you direct energy there and experience expansion.

Withdraw the prana from your right leg and return it back to ajna; this means relaxation.

Go on supplying prana to the right leg from ajna through the right side of the back and right hip, down to the tips of your toes.

Withdraw the prana back to ajna; retain the breath there, also your consciousness.

Left leg: In the same way, supply prana to the left leg, all the way to the tips of the toes.

Supply and expand; withdraw and relax.

All the prana comes from ajna and returns to ajna.

Bring your prana back to ajna and pause.

Right chest: Supply prana to the right side of your chest; withdraw it from the right side of your chest to ajna.
Supply and expand; withdraw with relax.
Bring your prana back to ajna, retain and pause.

Left chest: Avoiding the heart muscle, supply prana from ajna to the left side of your chest.
Withdraw the prana from the left side of your chest back to ajna.
Supply and expand; withdraw and relax.

Abdomen: Supply prana from ajna to the whole abdominal region.
Withdraw the prana from the whole abdominal region back to ajna.
Supply and expand; withdraw and relax.
Continue until distribution has been completed for all areas of the body.

Stage 6: Returning prana to mooladhara

When all distribution is complete, withdraw the prana back to ajna.
On the exhalation, take the prana down along the sushumna nadi from ajna to mooladhara and leave it there.
Do this with awareness.
Continue until all the prana has been returned to its source at mooladhara.

Stage 7: Ending the practice

Once complete, release khechari mudra and the ujjayi breath.
Bring the awareness to the natural breath moving in and out of the body.
Focus on the natural rhythm of the breath.
Notice parts of the body moving with the breath: the abdomen, chest, parts of the back.
Feel the breath contained within the physical body.
Shift the awareness fully to the physical body.
Be aware of the shape and form of the body.
Feel the contact of body with the floor.

Become aware of the space surrounding the body.
Have a sense of the room you are in.
Visualize the details of the room and your place within it.
Check that the senses are active and functioning normally.
Be aware of sounds around you, the places where the body touches the floor, smells, and tastes in the mouth.
Check that the awareness is fully externalized.
The practice is now complete.
When you are ready, gently open the eyes.

Hari Om Tat Sat

Practice note: Sometimes, when distributing prana to an organ or part of the body, the sensation of expansion and relaxation is felt indirectly through the heartbeat. When concentrating on charging a particular part of the body, it may happen that the practitioner will become aware of a pulse beat. The experience can be a little unusual at first; it is similar to expansion and relaxation, but there is total absorption in the pulse beat. The thump . . . thump . . . thump . . . of the pulse takes possession of the entire awareness, not just the sound of it, but the sensation of expansion and relaxation within it. This happens particularly when distributing prana to the lower extremities of the body. If this happens, just watch the experience; it will dissolve after a while.

PRACTICE 2: EXPANSION AND CONTRACTION

Stage 1: Preparation

Sit in an asana of your choice.

Alternatively, you may lie down, stand up or sit in a chair.

It is important that the body be comfortable and still throughout the practice, with the spine straight. However, if you need to move, do so slowly and with awareness, and then come back to stillness.

Make any final adjustments to the position of the body and then become still and quiet.

For a few moments, allow the body to settle.

Let any thoughts fade into the distance and let go of any physical or mental tension.

Shift the focus to the natural breath.

Be totally aware of the rhythm of the breath.

Be conscious of each incoming and outgoing breath.

Stage 2: Awakening and raising prana

Begin the practice of ujjayi pranayama.

Once ujjayi becomes effortless, begin to trace the path of pingala nadi with the breath.

On the inhalation, breath and awareness ascend from mooladhara to ajna.

On exhalation, the awareness and breath descend from ajna and return to mooladhara.

Continue following the path of pingala with the ujjayi breath.

When a steady rhythm has been established, visualize the movement of prana in tandem with the breath and awareness.

Streams of white light ascending and descending up and down the psychic passage of pingala.

Awareness completely immersed in the flowing white light of prana.

Next, begin to deposit the awakened prana at ajna.

At the end of each inhalation, pause for a few moments, storing prana in ajna. During exhalation, only the awareness descends back down to mooladhara.

Prana ascends along pingala and is deposited at ajna, the storehouse of prana, and only the awareness returns back to mooladhara.

Continue in this manner, building the storehouse of prana at ajna.

Stage 3: Expansion and contraction

Once sufficient energy has been stored, maintain the awareness at ajna for a few breaths and experience this concentration of prana in the form of light.

Now shift the awareness to the ujjayi pranayama and begin to develop the experience of expansion and contraction of the pranic body.

On the ujjayi inhalation, the pranic body expands; on the ujjayi exhalation, the pranic body contracts.

Continue to develop the awareness of this pranic and psychic expansion and contraction in synchrony with the ujjayi pranayama.

Stage 4: Distribution

Once established in expansion and contraction begin to distribute prana to different parts of the body.

Right arm: Supply prana to the right arm and expand it.

Withdraw prana from the right arm, returning it back to ajna and contract it.

Go on practising.

Left arm: Inhale, supply prana to the left arm and expand it.

Withdraw the prana, return it to ajna and contract.

Distributing from ajna and returning back to ajna; supply-expand, withdraw-contract.

Withdraw your prana back to ajna; retain the breath and prana in ajna for a few seconds and mentally relax the left arm.

Right leg: From ajna go through the right side of the back and hip to the right leg, the whole leg, right down to the tips of the toes.

Supply prana and feel the expansion; withdraw prana and feel the contraction.

Withdraw your prana back to ajna, retain the breath and prana here and relax the right leg mentally.

Left leg: Expand the left leg with prana.

Withdraw the prana from the left leg with contraction, back to ajna.

Supply prana from ajna through the left side of the back and hip to the left leg.

Withdraw the prana through the left hip and left side of the back and return to ajna.

Retain the prana in ajna and relax the left leg.

Abdomen: Supply prana to the whole abdominal region.

Supply and expand; withdraw and contract.

Distribution from ajna and returning back to ajna.

Withdraw your prana back to ajna, retain and relax the whole abdomen.

Right chest: Supply prana to the right side of the chest.

Supply and expand; withdraw and contract.

Distribution from ajna and returning back to ajna.

Withdraw your prana back to ajna, retain and relax the right side of the chest.

Left chest: Avoiding the heart muscle, supply prana and expand the left side of the chest.

Withdraw prana from the left side of the chest and contract again avoiding the heart muscle, returning back to ajna.

Supply from ajna; return to ajna.

Retain the prana in ajna for some time and relax the left side of the chest.

Brain: Expand and relax; then withdraw and contract.

In contraction, the cerebral portion is contracted to such an extent that there is no difference between the centre of the brain and any part of the circumference.

The brain is contracted to a point into the centre.

Then it is expanded to the shape of a ball, then contracted again to a point.

This is sometimes a difficult practice.

It takes time to experience contraction to a point.

When this is achieved, prana can be distributed to the cerebral area.
When expanding, relaxing or contracting the cerebral region, a headache may develop, some sort of heaviness may be experienced; if so, stop immediately.
Other than this there is no harm in distributing to the cerebral region.

Stage 5: Returning prana to mooladhara

When all distribution is concluded, withdraw the prana, returning it to ajna.
Then, take it down to mooladhara on the exhalation, following the sushumna passage, and leave it there.
Continue until all the prana has been returned to mooladhara.

Stage 6: Ending the practice

When finished, release both khechari mudra and ujjayi pranayama.
Shift the awareness to the natural breath moving in and out of the body.
Focus on the natural rhythm of the breath.
Notice parts of the body moving with the breath; the abdomen, chest, parts of the back.
Feel the breath contained within the physical body.
Shift the awareness from the breath to the physical body.
Experience the weight of the body in the chosen posture.
Be aware of the placement of the arms, the legs, the trunk, neck and head.
Be aware of the shape and form of the body.
Extend the awareness beyond the body and recall the room around you.
Visualize the details of the room and your place within the room.
Check that the senses are active and functioning normally.
Be aware of sounds around you, the touch of the body with the floor, smells and tastes within the mouth.
Check that the awareness is fully externalized.

The practice is now complete.
When you are ready, gently open the eyes.

Hari Om Tat Sat

EXTERNAL DISTRIBUTION

Practice note: When you begin external distribution, you may still be relying on your imagination or mental powers for visualization. This will lead to a mental experience only. However, once you have awakened the experience of prana, the streaks of light will become very vivid and you will have a direct pranic experience. Prana can be distributed in all directions outside the body. There are no restrictions in this regard. After mastering internal distribution, external distribution may be applied by those who wish to send prana to other individuals or simply to charge the environment around them

PRACTICE 3: EXPANSION AND RELAXATION

Stage 1: Preparation

Come into an asana of your choice.
If necessary, you may practise lying down, standing up or sitting in a chair.
Most importantly, check that the body is comfortable and at ease and the spine is straight.
For a few moments allow the body to settle and to become still and quiet.
Focus completely on the body and allow any thoughts to recede into the background.
Allow the body and mind to relax and let go of any physical or mental tension.
Commence ujjayi pranayama and khechari mudra.
Follow the soft, subtle sound of ujjayi and allow the awareness to internalize.

Stage 2: Awakening and raising prana

Continue with breath awareness and simultaneously develop an awareness of pingala nadi.

Begin to follow the breath and the awareness along pingala.

On the inhalation the breath ascends, mooladhara to ajna, and on the exhalation the breath descends, ajna to mooladhara.

Now visualize the movement of prana as it moves up and down pingala.

Streams of white light ascending and descending along pingala nadi.

Awareness and breath follow the flowing white light of prana.

Continue for some time.

Now begin to deposit the awakened prana at ajna.

At the end of each inhalation, pause for a few moments storing prana in ajna, and then descend only the awareness back to mooladhara with the exhalation.

Prana ascends through pingala to ajna, the storehouse of prana.

Only the awareness and breath return back to mooladhara.

Go on building up the storehouse of prana at ajna.

Once sufficient energy has been stored, hold your awareness at ajna and experience the bright light of prana.

Stage 3: External distribution

Visualize now a triangle or a circle around your body, or a cross that passes through your body.

The visualization should be luminous.

This *yantra*, or geometric shape, provides a protective shield for the body.

The prana can now be stretched in all directions outside the body without limit.

If it is just mental, it will only be a mental experience.

If it is actually the prana, the streaks of light will become very clear.

Initially, the practice will be a mental one.
Using the technique of expansion and relaxation, begin to expand prana outwards beyond the body.
With every ujjayi breath, intensify the experience of expansion and relaxation.
Visualize stretching the prana in all directions.
Stretch the prana at will, starting from ajna.
With every inhalation the prana expands from ajna, and with every exhalation, the prana relaxes back to ajna.
Go on expanding prana out beyond the body and into the environment.
Practise up to 49 rounds.

Stage 4: Returning prana to mooladhara

When the practice is complete, withdraw the prana back to ajna and be aware of ujjayi pranayama.
Check that all prana has been withdrawn to ajna.
Visualize once more the protective yantra surrounding the body.
Now prepare to return the prana to mooladhara, to its source.
On the next exhalation take the prana back down to mooladhara.
Return only the awareness to ajna, pause for a moment, and then return the prana back down to mooladhara.
Do this with awareness and continue until all the prana has been returned to mooladhara.

Stage 5: Ending the practice

Release khechari mudra and ujjayi pranayama.
Shift the awareness to the natural breath moving in and out of the body.
Focus on the natural rhythm of the breath.
Be aware of the physical body containing the breath.
Feel the body in the chosen posture or position.
Be aware of the sensations of the body.
Extend the awareness and have a sense of the space that surrounds the body.

Visualize the details of the room and your place within the room.
Check that the senses are active and functioning normally.
Be aware of sounds around you, the touch of the parts of the body with the chair or floor, be aware of smells, and the tastes within the mouth.
Check that the awareness is fully externalized.
The practice is now complete.
If you wish, practise palming and gently open the eyes.

Hari Om Tat Sat

PRACTICE 4: EXPANSION AND CONTRACTION

Stage 1: Preparation

In this practice the prana is distributed externally to purify and energize the environment.
Sit in a comfortable, meditative posture or lie down in shavasana.
Make yourself comfortable and still.
Allow the body and mind to become calm and peaceful.
If you are sitting, make sure your body weight is equally distributed on each side.
Begin to observe your breathing process.
As you breathe in and out, totally relax the body.
Become perfectly motionless.
Tell yourself mentally, "I shall not move throughout the duration of the practice. I shall remain aware and alert."
Remember that you should not break the flow of awareness; there should be no wavering of your concentration.

Stage 2: Awakening and raising prana

Become aware of the inner body space.
Within the space, visualize the spinal passage and the chakras.
Develop an intense awareness of pingala nadi.

Then synchronize the ujjayi breath with awareness of pingala and fold the tongue back into khechari mudra.

As you breathe in, the breath rises from mooladhara to ajna along pingala.

As you breathe out, the breath descends straight down sushumna from ajna to mooladhara.

Experience the movement of prana in pingala nadi.

Visualize it in the form of a rapid stream of luminous, blue-white or golden light.

Direct the prana with your breath and awareness up along pingala nadi from mooladhara to ajna.

Retain the breath at ajna for five seconds repeating mentally, 'ajna, ajna, ajna, ajna, ajna'.

Then, while exhaling, bring only the breath and awareness back down to mooladhara through sushumna nadi, leaving the prana stored at ajna.

Continue awakening the prana along pingala nadi with absolute concentration, feeling the energy movement intensely.

Continue this practice until the actual awakening of prana is experienced.

In the beginning, practise up to 49 rounds.

When you have mastered the practice, you will feel the awakening of prana clearly.

Stage 3: Distribution of prana

Having raised the prana carefully and systematically to ajna chakra, focus your full concentration there and see the bright pranic glow.

Feel the build-up of stored energy in this chakra.

Next, begin to form a protective luminous circle or upward pointing triangle around the body, or you can also see a luminous cross passing through the body.

When you can clearly see one of these luminous shapes around the body, feel that you are protected by it.

Breathe in with ujjayi and khechari; visualize streaks of pranic light saturating your body and emanating outwards filling the shape around you with light.

Using your willpower, begin to expand the prana in all directions, or you can send it out in one particular direction if you wish.

With the exhalation, as the prana withdraws back to the storehouse at ajna, experience a definite *bandha* or contraction there.

This intensifies the experience and makes the following emission of prana more powerful.

First the pranic light fills the circle, triangle or cross protecting your physical body.

Continue for some time sending the prana out to fill this geometric shape and bringing it back to contract at ajna.

Then see the prana expanding beyond the shape to fill the room in which you are practising.

See pranic light floating through the whole room and expanding outwards with brilliant light rays every time you inhale.

Exhale and withdraw the prana back to ajna and feel a definite contraction at that chakra.

As you continue inhaling and exhaling with ujjayi, see the prana expand out further and further.

Continue with this experience for some time.

Feel your environment being purified and energized.

Stage 4: Returning prana to mooladhara

To end the practice, withdraw back the prana to ajna and hold the awareness at that chakra for some time while practising ujjayi pranayama.

Check that you have returned all your prana to ajna.

Become aware of the luminous circle, triangle or cross which you have defined around your physical body.

Visualize your body confined by this luminous shape.

Now prepare to return the prana to mooladhara, to its source.

On the next exhalation, take the prana back down through sushumna nadi to mooladhara.

Return only the breath and awareness to ajna, pause for a moment, and then return the prana, breath and awareness back down mooladhara.

Do this with awareness and continue until all the prana has been returned to mooladhara.

Stage 5: Ending the practice

Release khechari mudra and discontinue ujjayi pranayama.

Become aware of the natural breath moving within the body.

Experience the physical body in the chosen posture.

Be aware of the placement of the arms and legs, head, neck and spine.

Feel the contact of the floor beneath the body and the sensation this creates.

Become attuned to the environment surrounding the body; the sounds near and far, the temperature of the air on the skin.

Recall the details of the room, the time of day, the colour of the clothes you are wearing.

Ensure that the senses have been externalized completely and are functioning normally; the sense of taste, smell, touch, hearing.

If necessary, practise a few more rounds of returning prana to mooladhara.

Once satisfied that the senses are intact, make small movements and gently open the eyes.

The practice is now complete.

Hari Om Tat Sat

VISION OF PRANA SHAKTI

PRACTICE 5: VISION OF PRANA SHAKTI

Stage 1: Preparation

Prepare for the practice by lying in shavasana.
Allow the whole body and mind to become still and steady.
Let the body completely surrender to the floor.
Let the floor support the weight of the body.
Consciously let go of any tension: physical, mental or emotional.
Whole body relaxed and at ease.
Become aware of the natural breath moving with the body.
Notice each and every inhalation and exhalation.
Follow the natural breath for some time, allowing all tension to dissolve and the mind to become still.

Stage 2: Dissolving the body

Prepare now to dissolve the body.
To begin, take your awareness to the right big toe.
Obtain a clear and accurate inner vision of the big toe.
Now visualize the right big toe gradually melting or dissolving like a lump of butter which has been placed close to a fire.
Watch it slowly lose its form and disperse.
Gradually let it melt or dissolve completely.
Actually feel your big toe dissolving.
Now practise melting or dissolving each of the toes on the right foot.
Once you can do this, begin to dissolve the other parts of the body in sequence.
Progressively imagine each and every part of the body to be melting and dissolving totally.
From the toes, the whole right foot dissolves with the awareness.
Continue to melt the body from the right ankle up the right leg to the right hip.

The whole right leg melting and dissolving.
Melt the physical notion of the body into nothing.
Shift the awareness to the left foot and the toes.
Begin to dissolve each of the toes one by one.
In the same way, continue to dissolve the whole left foot and leg up to the left hip.
If streaks of brilliant blue-white light appear it means that prana is manifesting.
The awareness of the physical body is dissolving into awareness of the pranic body.
Continue this until the form of pranamaya kosha is spontaneously experienced.
Shift the focus to the pelvic region and begin to dissolve the whole pelvis, the abdomen and the chest, both right and left side.
The whole torso melting and dissolving with the awareness.
From the right shoulder, begin to dissolve the whole right arm down to the right hand.
Systematically dissolve the fingers one by one until the whole right hand and arm have disappeared.
Shift the awareness to the left shoulder and again gradually melt the whole left arm down to the fingers of the left hand.
Move now to the neck and the head, and experience them dissolving in a wave of warmth, like wax melting in the heat of the candle flame.
For a few moments experience the pranic body, free from the limitations of the physical body, the physical structure.
The whole pranic body glowing with particles of light, the vision of prana shakti.

Stage 3: Ending the practice

Release the vision of prana shakti and connect with the natural breath.
Experience the sensation of the incoming and outgoing breath.

Feel the sensation of the breath at the nostrils, the coolness of the breath on the inhalation and the warmth of the breath on the exhalation.
Deepen the breath slightly and become aware of the movement of the breath in the chest and abdomen.
Feel the slight expansion of abdomen and chest on inhalation and the relaxation on exhalation.
Expand the awareness of the physical body to include the arms, legs, the whole torso, neck and head.
Be aware of the whole body.
Feel the weight and solidity of the physical body.
Feel the solidity of the ground beneath the body, supporting the body in shavasana.
Have a sense now of the space surrounding the physical body.
Remember the room in which you are lying, and your place within the room.
Listen to the sounds, inside and outside the room.
Allow these sounds to externalize the awareness completely.
Draw the awareness back into the physical body and prepare mentally to move the body.
Become aware of the toes and the fingers and begin to move them slowly.
Move the head from side to side, and stretch the arms up overhead.
When you are ready slowly sit up.
If you wish, practise palming and then gently open the eyes.
The practice is now complete.

Hari Om Tat Sat

Practice note: This practice can be commenced at any part of the body, although usually it starts with the right hand thumb or big toe. The practice is best done over a few days or weeks. It has to be practised step by step and the psychic sensation controlled. Each and every part of the body is progressively dissolved.

Ultimately a light body is realized. It can happen at any time. For a small fraction of a second it is possible to view the luminous body of prana shakti. At this point the awareness has moved beyond both the physical and the psychic dimension and into the pranic dimension directly. The vision of prana shakti can come to certain sensitive people as soon as they start dissolving the toes. It can happen to anyone at any stage in the process of dissolution. Once this vision is successfully achieved the distribution of prana becomes more effective.

15

Self-Healing

FORMING OR STRENGTHENING A HEALING SANKALPA

Practice 1: Yoga nidra for a healing sankalpa

GENERAL HEALTH: WHOLE BODY DISTRIBUTION

Practice 2: Expansion and relaxation
Practice 3: Expansion and contraction

HEALING DAMAGED PARTS OR SYSTEMS

Practice 4: Awakening prana for healing
Practice 5: Awakening prana for healing (variation)

For healing practices to be effective, it is necessary to have awakened the vision of prana shakti. Charging one's own body or that of another with prana should only take place once the healer or practitioner has experienced genuine pranic awakening. Healing can only happen through the pranic body; visualization at the mental level is not sufficient. Prana must be visualized easily, and at will, as a flow of light particles. Thus for healing to be successful, each stage must be performed effortlessly with one-pointed concentration.

This chapter contains a specialized yoga nidra that guides the awareness into a more subtle exploration of the illness or pain, and facilitates the creation of a holistic healing sankalpa. The overall healing sankalpa may be a positive resolve to be fit and healthy, to be full of vitality or to experience complete wellbeing. However, this practice also aims at discovering any physical, mental or emotional factors that may prevent healing and to make a series of practical sankalpas, giving a practical direction for health. This practice can be repeated until the ideal sankalpa has been formed and achieved.

Also contained in this chapter are practices for self-healing, divided into two sections. The first section is for maintaining or restoring general health. In these practices, prana is distributed to different parts of the body systematically and then to the whole body. The second section awakens prana for healing physical injuries or illnesses such as broken bones, sprains, slipped disc, arthritis, weak or diseased organs. Prana is consciously directed to the relevant part again and again. The specific area is saturated with prana and then it is distributed to the whole body.

FORMING OR STRENGTHENING A HEALING SANKALPA

PRACTICE 1: YOGA NIDRA FOR A HEALING SANKALPA

Stage 1: Preparation

Lie down in shavasana; ensure that your head, neck, spine, trunk and legs are in a straight line.

The feet are about 45 cms apart; the arms are slightly away from the sides of the body with the palms facing upwards.

Allow the fingers to curl naturally in towards the palms.

The eyes and the mouth are gently closed.

Completely relax the whole body; check that there are no points of tension.

Stop all physical movement and be aware of the complete stillness of the body.

Do this with the attitude of a witness, a silent observer observing the stillness of the body.

Become aware of all the different external sounds around you.

For a few minutes move your awareness from one sound to the next without analyzing the sounds intellectually.

Be a witness only.

Now mentally visualize the environment around you and see your body as though you are looking at it from outside.

Focus your attention on the natural and spontaneous flow of breath for several minutes.

Carefully follow its path from the opening of the nostrils, down the throat, into the lungs and out again.

Maintain unbroken awareness of each and every breath without even a fraction of a break.

Be a witness to your effortless, spontaneous breathing.

After a few minutes tell yourself mentally, "I will not sleep. I will remain awake throughout the practice."

Stage 2: Sankalpa

If you already have a healing *sankalpa*, resolve, repeat it three times with faith and conviction.

If you have not yet made a sankalpa, keep an open mind throughout the practice so that you can formulate one for the next time.

Stage 3: Rotation of awareness and prana

Now rotate your consciousness through the body.

Let your awareness flow from one part of the body to the next as it is named, feeling the energy moving with the awareness.

Take your awareness to the right side of the body, the right hand thumb, first finger, second finger, third finger, fourth finger, palm of the hand, back of the hand, wrist, lower arm, elbow, upper arm, shoulder, armpit, waist, hip, right thigh, knee, calf muscle, ankle, heel, sole, top of the foot, right big toe, second toe, third toe, fourth toe, fifth toe.

Now bring your awareness to the left side, left hand thumb, first finger, second finger, third finger, fourth finger, palm of the hand, back of the hand, wrist, lower arm, elbow, upper arm, shoulder, armpit, waist, hip, left thigh, knee, calf muscle, ankle, heel, sole, top of the foot, left big toe, second toe, third toe, fourth toe, fifth toe.

Move the awareness and energy now to the back of the body, moving from part to part: right shoulder, left shoulder, right shoulder blade, left shoulder blade, right buttock, left buttock, the spine, the whole of the back, the back of the neck and the back of the head.

To the front of the body: the top of the head, forehead, right eyebrow, left eyebrow, the eyebrow centre, right eyelid, left eyelid, right eye, left eye, right ear, left ear, right cheek, left cheek, nose, tip of the nose, right nostril, left nostril, upper lip, lower lip, chin, jaw, throat, right collarbone, left collarbone, right side of the chest, left side of the chest, middle of the chest, navel, abdomen, lower abdomen, pelvic region.

Whole of the right leg, whole of the left leg, both legs together.

Whole of the right arm, whole of the left arm, both arms together.

Whole of the back, whole of the front, whole of the head, and all together.

Legs, arms, back, front, head; the whole body, the whole body, the whole physical body.

Be aware of yourself as the witness of the whole body.

I am not this body, I am not this mind, I am the witness.

Stage 4: Visualization of the part to be healed

Begin focusing your awareness on the exact location of the part or parts to be healed.

Go right inside the body mentally and see the area or organ.

Visualize the exact shape and size of the affected part.
When you have a clear picture of it, start to move your awareness slowly around and inside it, seeing it in as much detail as possible; see the related muscles and bones, the tissues, nerves, cells and blood; see what colour it is.
Examine the particular organ or area from all possible angles.

Stage 5: Exploring the disorder

Now become aware of any pain emanating from the injured or diseased part; be very aware of the extent, depth and quality of the pain.
Focus your full attention on it as you visualize this part.
Examine whether the pain is continuous or intermittent, dull or sharp.
Is the pain static or moving?
Does it throb in one specific place or shoot through the body?
Take a careful note of all related feelings and sensations.
Examine the pain carefully, noticing it as a witness.
Next, try to find out the underlying cause of the pain.
Relax and take your time.
Assess the extent of the problem deep within the body and mind; be fully aware of any underlying weakness or illness.
Be aware also of the cause which was the catalyst for creating it.
As well as you can, ascertain which system or systems of the body are involved from among the digestive, cardiovascular, respiratory, immune, endocrine, nervous, reproductive, limbic, excretory, lymphatic and skeleto-muscular systems.
Go on intensifying your *antar trataka,* or inner concentration, on the physical part or organ, on the pain, and on any associated sickness or damage.

Stage 6: Contemplating healing

Once antar trataka has been firmly established, begin to focus on the change you wish to occur in your body.

Be fully aware of which systems you need to bring into balance in order to affect a cure.

If necessary, establish a system and schedule of repair.

Now begin to examine your desire for a cure.

Do you sincerely wish to be healed?

Perhaps part of your suffering has its origin in your thinking pattern or maybe you need to change your lifestyle.

Maybe you are negative about yourself or have a negative approach to life in general.

Be completely honest with yourself.

Sometimes sickness or pain can be a means to avoid situations we find too unpleasant to face.

Try to be aware if this is the case.

If it is, your healing resolve will need to incorporate this aspect of your suffering.

To heal fully you must come to terms with the psychic or emotional patterns that keep you ill before you can successfully approach the physical symptoms.

As the mind thinks, so the body reflects.

Try to assess your own willingness to change.

Is your mind currently willing to bring about a cure, or must you heal the mental level first?

Know how strong your desire for a cure actually is.

If you realize that your physical health is undermined by negative psychological patterns, add the healing of this deeper dimension to your system of repairs.

Basically, your sankalpa, your resolve, needs to be wholeheartedly positive and sincere; only then will the healing work begin to take deep and speedy effect.

Stage 7: Healing sankalpa

You should take time to carefully formulate a healing sankalpa or resolve based on your system of repairs.

The resolve in yoga nidra is powerful and comes true in your life.

This sankalpa should be simple, practical and precise.

If you realize several adjustments have to be made, be practical and begin with the first.

For example, an adjustment of diet, attitude or friends.
Once you have succeeded with that, proceed to the second.
In this way your faith in the practice will increase until you have absolute faith that the process will succeed.
If you have already formulated your resolve, repeat it three times.

Stage 8: Ending the practice

Having made your sankalpa, bring your awareness back to the body and to its position in the room.
Develop homogeneous awareness of the whole body lying in shavasana.
Become aware of the whole body in relation to the floor.
Feel all the meeting points between your body and the floor.
Become aware of the meeting points between the back of your head and the floor, shoulder blades and the floor, the elbows and the floor, backs of the hands and the floor, the buttocks and the floor, calf muscles and the floor, the heels and the floor.
Be aware of all these meeting points between the body and the floor simultaneously, a line of contact, a plane of contact between the body and the floor, between the floor and the body.
Extend the awareness beyond the body and recall the room you are in.
Mentally visualize all the details of the room and your position within it.
Listen to the sounds in the environment and allow these sounds to bring you into the present moment.
Know that you have been practising yoga nidra and the practice is now complete.
Be aware fully of the physical body.
Begin to make small movements.
Move the fingers and the toes, arms and the legs.
Move the head gently from side to side.

Stretch the arms up overhead and give the whole body a good stretch.
When you are ready, gradually sit up and open the eyes.

Hari Om Tat Sat

GENERAL HEALTH: WHOLE BODY DISTRIBUTION

PRACTICE 2: EXPANSION AND RELAXATION

Stage 1: Preparation

Assume a comfortable posture.
The prana will be distributed internally so it is recommended that you either sit with the legs outstretched or lie down in shavasana.
If you are sitting up, make sure your body weight is equally distributed on both sides.
Relax the whole body completely.
Begin to observe your breathing process.
As you breathe in and out, totally relax the body.
Remember that you should not move the body at all during the practice.
The flow of awareness should not be broken, so tell yourself firmly, 'I shall remain awake and attentive until the practice is complete. I shall not sleep.'

Stage 2: Tracing pingala nadi

Become aware of the body as a hollow shell and observe the inner space.
Within the space, visualize the spinal passage and the chakras.
Develop an intense awareness of pingala nadi and visualize it curving from mooladhara to the right, from swadhisthana to the left, from manipura to the right, from anahata to the left, from vishuddhi to the right and coming to ajna.
From ajna, bring your awareness straight down sushumna to mooladhara and begin the next round.

Synchronize the breath with the movement of prana and consciousness in pingala nadi.

The form of the breath is ujjayi and the tongue is folded gently back into khechari mudra.

As you breathe in, the prana rises from mooladhara to ajna along pingala nadi.

As you breathe out, the prana descends in a straight line down sushumna from ajna to mooladhara.

Stage 3: Raising prana to ajna

Now begin to experience the movement of prana flowing up pingala nadi.

Visualize prana in the form of a stream of blue-white light moving like an electric current.

On the ujjayi inhalation, move the breath and awareness along with the prana curving up through pingala from mooladhara to ajna chakra.

Retain the breath at ajna for five seconds repeating mentally, 'ajna, ajna, ajna, ajna, ajna'.

Then, while exhaling, just bring the awareness back down to mooladhara through sushumna nadi; the prana remains at ajna.

Continue the practice until the actual awakening of prana is experienced.

Continue awakening the prana along pingala nadi with absolute concentration, feeling the movement of energy intensely and visualizing the prana vividly.

In the beginning you should practise 49 rounds.

Later, when you have mastered the practicc, you will not have to count the rounds because you will feel the awakening of prana.

Stage 4: Distributing prana to the whole body

Now, when you reach ajna chakra, remain there in antar kumbhaka for a few seconds without strain.

Then exhale, not down sushumna, but through every pore of the body, like a sponge releasing water, and relax your whole body.

Again with the inhalation, breathe in through every pore and cell, and feel the whole body expand like a balloon.
Go on experiencing relaxation with every exhalation and expansion with every inhalation.
Remember you are breathing in ujjayi pranayama.
The ujjayi breath is experienced throughout the body as if every pore and cell is sucking in prana.
When you inhale, every pore and cell breathes in and the whole body expands like a balloon.
When you exhale, your whole body breathes out and relaxes totally, like a rag doll.
Increase this awareness of the whole body breathing, of the whole body expanding upon inhalation and relaxing upon exhalation.
Bring your awareness back to ajna chakra, the storehouse for the distribution of prana.
Ajna is now the focal point for the entire breathing process; the beginning and the end of the process of inhaling and exhaling, expanding and relaxing, is at ajna chakra.
Inhalation expands out through the body from ajna and exhalation withdraws back to ajna.
Inhale from ajna and distribute the prana throughout the body from the top of the head to the tips of the toes.
Experience the whole body as if it were an inflatable balloon.
During exhalation withdraw the prana back to ajna and experience complete relaxation.
Inhale, distribute and expand; exhale, withdraw and relax.
This is the process and form of your awareness now.
Be totally alert.
With absolute concentration, continue with this steady rhythm; inhale, distribute and expand; exhale, withdraw and relax.
Maintain ujjayi, and from time to time you may need to relax khechari mudra for a few moments and then return to it.

Continue with awareness of ajna chakra, the storehouse from where the prana is being distributed to the entire body with the help of ujjayi, and to which prana is withdrawn back again.

Ujjayi pranayama should become spontaneous and natural so that during the process of distribution and withdrawal of prana, the breathing goes on by itself, effortlessly.

You must be able to apply your concentration totally to the vision of prana, to the movement of prana and to the experience of distribution and expansion, withdrawal and relaxation.

Although you are breathing in and out, there is only the awareness of distribution and expansion, withdrawal and relaxation.

Continue this practice with total awareness, total mental alertness.

When you inhale, distribute the prana from ajna in all directions, filling the entire body with luminous light streaks, and experience expansion.

When you exhale, withdraw the prana from all parts of the body back to ajna and experience relaxation.

The breathing is natural and spontaneous.

Your awareness follows the rhythmic process of distribution and expansion, withdrawal and relaxation.

Inhaling, extend the pranic force to all parts of the body.

Exhaling, bring it back to its source at ajna.

At the time of distribution, feel that your whole body is saturated inside and outside with dynamic pranic energy.

As you withdraw, feel the body relaxing.

Develop the experience of total void, *shoonyata*, in the body.

Within this void, see the light force shooting rapidly throughout the body.

Stage 5: Distribution to individual body parts

Now focus on the individual body parts.

As you inhale, direct the prana from ajna to the right arm and feel it expand.

Extend your awareness into the right arm only.
Feel the prana entering into each and every cell of the right arm from the shoulders down to the fingertips, filling up each and every part of the right arm.
Visualize the right arm as luminous and bright; feel it expanding with light.
As you exhale, withdraw the prana from the right arm back to ajna.
Experience the right arm relaxing.
Continue for some time, filling up the right arm with prana and expanding the energy psychically, then withdrawing the prana back to ajna and relaxing the right arm.
The processes of expansion and relaxation are entirely pranic; there is no actual, physical movement.
Feel the prana flowing from ajna to the right arm and back again intensely.
Now take your awareness to the left arm.
Distribute the prana throughout the left arm from the shoulder to the fingertips.
As you distribute the prana, feel the expansion of the left arm.
Fill the whole arm, both inside and outside, with dazzling light.
Feel that each and every cell, tissue, muscle and bone is pervaded with awareness of prana, the experience of prana.
As you exhale, withdraw the energy and relax.
With every supply and withdrawal of prana you are expanding and relaxing the vital force, the energy in the left arm.
Now bring your awareness to the right leg.
Distribute prana throughout the right leg, seeing it fill up with pranic energy. Distribute and expand; withdraw and relax.
Be totally aware of the right leg only.
Intensify the awareness of expansion and relaxation.

Feel the prana permeating each and every part of the right leg both inside and out.
Next become aware of the left leg.
Localize the awareness of prana to the left leg.
Distribute prana throughout the left leg from the hip down to the toes; distribute and expand, withdraw and relax.
Be aware of the left leg only.
Intensify the awareness of expansion and relaxation.
Feel prana permeating each and every part of the left leg, both inside and outside, see it glow with luminous energy.
Continue for some time.
Now focus your attention at the lower abdomen, from the navel down to the perineum.
The process of breathing is gentle, spontaneous ujjayi.
Begin to supply prana to all the organs in the lower abdomen: the small intestine, the large intestine, the bowels, the bladder, the urinary organ and the excretory organs. Feel the prana pervading the whole lower abdomen and expanding.
Withdraw the prana and relax, bringing your awareness back to ajna chakra.
Concentrate on the upper abdomen where many important organs are situated.
Inhale, supply and expand; exhale, withdraw and relax.
Use the full power of your awareness; feel the prana filling each and every cell, tissue, nerve and organ, see the stomach filling with prana and expanding.
Visualize the spleen, the liver, the pancreas and the kidneys filling with prana and expanding.
With each exhalation, withdraw the prana back to ajna and relax totally.
Now become aware of the chest from the diaphragm to the throat and continue the same process: inhale, supply and expand; exhale, withdraw and relax.
Visualize the lungs filling with prana and expanding, but do not supply prana to the heart directly.

Expand the whole chest with prana, see both inside and out becoming luminous and bright with pranic energy, then exhale and withdraw the prana back to ajna.

Finally, supply prana to the head.

Experience the sensation of the prana radiating from ajna chakra throughout the brain and head on inhalation.

With exhalation, feel the prana again moving back to ajna chakra.

Inhale and distribute prana within the head to each and every part of the brain, to the sensory organs: the eyes, the ears, the nose and the tongue; to the face and all the facial muscles; to every cell and tissue within the head.

Distribution happens at the time of inhalation and relaxation at the time of exhalation.

Stage 6: Light body

Ajna is the storehouse of prana, experienced as infinite light streaks.

Each time you inhale, streaks of light particles issue forth with lightning velocity like molten lava shooting forth during a volcanic eruption.

Make the experience vivid and intense.

Experience white light radiating from ajna inside the head at the time of distribution and on exhalation experience the withdrawal of energy back to ajna.

Develop this awareness to the maximum.

Now become aware of the whole body.

Begin to distribute prana to the whole body and feel the pranic body expand.

Visualize white light emanating from ajna like light streaks shooting forth from fireworks and pervading the whole body.

Relax and withdraw, again experiencing the white light returning to ajna.

Maintain complete awareness of the pranic energy pervading the whole body; each and every organ, muscle, atom and cell is illumined with energy.

Experience white light radiating from ajna and pervading the whole body inside and out.

Stage 7: Withdrawal of prana to mooladhara

Bring the awareness back to ajna chakra.

Withdraw all the pranic energies back to ajna and become aware of the ujjayi breathing.

Inhale and pause, holding the breath and awareness at ajna.

Exhale and take the breath, awareness and prana back down to mooladhara via sushumna nadi.

Continue to take the prana down to mooladhara very carefully and with absolute awareness.

When you reach mooladhara, deposit the prana there, then inhale and bring the awareness straight back up sushumna to ajna.

Hold the breath at ajna for a few seconds, exhale and take more prana down to mooladhara through sushumna.

Continue this practice until you are quite sure all the prana has been returned to mooladhara.

Stage 8: Ending the practice

Release khechari mudra and ujjayi pranayama. Allow the breath to return to normal.

Then, slowly and carefully begin to externalize your awareness.

Become aware of the outside sounds.

Mentally reconstruct the environment around you.

Focus on your breathing for a few minutes and come back fully into your physical body.

At this point your body should feel light and your awareness should be fully grounded in the present, physical moment.

Become aware of the position of your body either sitting or lying down.

Do not move the body immediately, just be aware of its position and the fact that you are about to move or sit up.

For a few seconds check that your awareness has

returned to normal and that you are in conscious control of your faculties.

Check the senses: sense of smell, taste, touch and hearing.

If, however, you find that you are not fully back in your physical body and in your normal state of functioning awareness, again take the awareness back to ajna.

Using ujjayi pranayama, repeat a few rounds of descending with the prana back down to mooladhara.

Once your awareness is fully externalized, slowly sit up, or release your asana, and open your eyes.

Hari Om Tat Sat

PRACTICE 3: EXPANSION AND CONTRACTION

Stage 1: Preparation

Come into a comfortable sitting position or lie down in shavasana.

Make yourself completely comfortable.

If you are sitting up, make sure your body weight is equally distributed on both sides.

Once you've made the final adjustments, let the body become still and steady.

Allow both the body and the mind to become calm and peaceful.

Begin to observe your breathing process.

As you breathe in and out, relax the body even further.

Complete stillness of body and mind.

Tell yourself mentally, 'I shall not move throughout the duration of the practice. I shall remain aware and alert.'

Stage 2: Awakening prana

Become aware of the inner body space.

Within the space visualize the spinal passage and the chakras.

Develop an intense awareness of pingala nadi.

Move the awareness up and down tracing the path of pingala nadi.

Then synchronize the awareness of pingala with ujjayi breathing, folding the tongue back into khechari mudra.
Begin to awaken and raise the prana.
As you breathe in, the prana rises from mooladhara to ajna along pingala.
As you breathe out, only the awareness descends straight down sushumna from ajna to mooladhara.
On inhalation, move the prana with your breath and awareness along pingala nadi from mooladhara to ajna.
Visualize it in the form of a rapid stream of light.
Retain the breath at ajna for five seconds repeating mentally, 'ajna, ajna, ajna, ajna, ajna'.
Then, while exhaling, bring just the awareness back down to mooladhara through sushumna nadi.
Continue awakening the prana along pingala nadi.
Practise up to 49 rounds.
When you have mastered the practice, the actual awakening of prana will be felt intuitively and counting the rounds will not be necessary.

Stage 3: Expanding and contracting the whole body

Now, when you reach ajna chakra remain there in kumbhaka for a few seconds.
Then exhale through every pore of the body, and feel your whole body contract psychically.
With every inhalation, breathe in through every pore and cell, and feel the whole body expand.
Go on experiencing contraction with every exhalation and expansion with every inhalation.
Feel the incoming ujjayi breath throughout the body, as if every pore of the skin is gently drawing in air.
When you inhale, every pore and cell of the body breathes in, and the whole body expands like a balloon.
When you exhale, your whole body breathes out and contracts.
Be aware of the body breathing as a single dynamic unit.
The whole body expands and contracts as one living organism.

Take your awareness back to ajna, the storehouse for the distribution of prana.
Ajna is now the focal point for the entire breathing process.
The beginning and end of the inhalation and exhalation, expansion and contraction process is at ajna.
Inhalation extends throughout the body from ajna while exhalation withdraws back to ajna.
From ajna, inhale and distribute prana throughout the body from the top of the head to the tip of the toes.
Experience the whole body expanding uniformly.
During exhalation, withdraw the prana back to ajna and experience psychic contraction; inhale, distribute and expand; exhale, withdraw and contract.
This is the form of your awareness now.
When you direct prana throughout the body, mentally feel it expanding in all directions.
It is a pranic and psychic expansion.
The whole body from head to toe is saturated with brilliant pranic force on the inhalation; feel and visualize this intensely.
Simultaneously, imagine that your psychic body is expanding extensively in all directions.
When you exhale, consciously withdraw your prana from all parts of the body and direct it back to ajna chakra.
Just as the water of the ocean recedes when the tidal flow is reversed, so prana recedes during exhalation and contraction takes place.
During this pranic and psychic contraction, body consciousness is transcended.
The body is expanded and contracted as one homogeneous unit.
Inhale, distribute, expand; exhale, withdraw, contract.
Be totally alert and continue for some time.

Stage 4: Distributing prana to individual body parts

Now we shall do the same practice focusing on individual body parts.

As you inhale, direct the prana to the right arm and feel it expand energetically and psychically; extend your awareness to the right arm only.
Feel the prana entering into each and every cell of the right arm from the shoulder down to the finger tips.
See the right arm glow with light.
As you exhale, withdraw the prana back to ajna and be aware of the right arm contracting.
Continue for a short time seeing the prana in the right arm becoming brighter and brighter.
Inhale, distribute and expand; exhale, withdraw back to ajna and contract.
Distribute the prana inside the arm and also experience the prana extending outside the arm in an aura of warmth and light.
Feel the movement of prana from ajna to the right arm, then return it back to ajna.
Now go to the left arm and as you inhale, distribute the prana throughout the left arm from shoulder to fingertips and be aware of the energy in the left arm expanding.
Feel the whole left arm, both inside and out, being pervaded with pranic light.
As you exhale, withdraw the prana back to ajna and experience contraction.
With every supply and withdrawal of prana, the energy field expands and contracts.
Move the awareness to the right leg.
Begin to distribute prana within the body; from ajna down the right side body to the hip, throughout the right leg and down to the toes.
Inhale, distribute and expand; exhale, withdraw and contract.
Be aware of the right leg only, to the exclusion of the rest of the body.
Intensify this experience of expansion and contraction.
The prana saturates each and every part of the right leg both inside and out.

See the right leg full of light.
Next, localize your awareness of prana in the left leg.
Distribute prana throughout the left leg, from the hip down to the toes, and expand it.
Withdraw the prana and feel the left leg contract.
Increase your awareness of expansion and contraction.
Feel the prana permeating each and every atom of the left leg both inside and out.
Focus now on the lower abdomen, from the navel down to the perineum.
Supply prana and expand; withdraw prana and contract.
Remember the whole process is psychic and pranic.
The breathing is spontaneous ujjayi pranayama.
Supply pranic energy to all the organs in the lower abdomen: the large intestine, the small intestine, the bowels, bladder, urinary organ and excretory organ.
Feel the whole lower abdomen vibrating with pranic light and expanding; then withdraw and contract, bringing your awareness back to ajna chakra.
Visualize the upper abdomen between the navel and the ribcage, and see it being energized by prana.
Inhale, supply and expand; exhale, withdraw and contract.
Intensify this awareness.
Feel the prana energizing each and every cell, tissue, nerve and organ.
See the stomach, the spleen, the pancreas, the liver, the kidneys all glowing with the vital energy of prana.
Exhale and contract; withdraw the prana back to ajna.
Now concentrate at the chest area, from the diaphragm to the throat.
Inhale, supply and expand; exhale, withdraw and contract.
Do not supply prana directly to the heart.
Visualize the lungs shining with prana and expanding.
Expand the whole chest area, except the heart, with prana.

See the whole chest, inside and out, becoming luminous and bright.

Exhale and withdraw the prana to ajna, but do not contract the chest psychically.

Finally, take your awareness to the head.

As you inhale, experience prana radiating from ajna chakra throughout the brain and head as the whole head expands.

With exhalation, feel the prana again returning to ajna chakra.

Inhale and distribute prana within the head to each and every part of the brain and sensory organs: the eyes, the ears, the nose and the tongue, to the face and facial muscles, to every cell and tissue within the head.

Experience expansion at the time of inhalation and contraction at the time of exhalation.

Stage 5: Light body

Become aware of the whole body.

Begin to distribute prana to the whole body and feel the pranic body expand.

Visualize light streaks shooting forth like they do from a big sparkler and pervading the whole body.

Exhale and again experience the white light returning to ajna.

Maintain complete awareness of the pranic energy permeating the whole body; each and every part being flooded with a stream of white light.

Stage 6: Returning prana to mooladhara

Bring the awareness back to ajna chakra.

Withdraw all the pranic energies back to ajna and become aware again of ujjayi pranayama.

Inhale and retain the breath for a short time, concentrating the awareness at ajna.

Exhale and take the prana back down to mooladhara via sushumna nadi.

Take the prana down to mooladhara very carefully and with absolute awareness.

When you reach mooladhara deposit the prana there, then inhale and bring the awareness straight back up sushumna to ajna.

Retain the breath at ajna for a few seconds, exhale, and take more prana down to mooladhara through sushumna.

Continue this practice until you are quite sure all the prana has been returned to mooladhara.

Stage 7: Ending the practice

Shift the awareness to the breath.

Release khechari mudra and the ujjayi pranayama; return to normal breathing.

Experience the rhythmical flow of the inhalation and exhalation.

Be aware of the breathing process occurring naturally within the body.

Feel the breath entering the nostrils and filling the lungs with air on inhalation.

On the exhalation, feel the lungs deflate and the breath exiting through the nostrils.

As you observe the breath allow the awareness to gradually externalize.

Feel the whole physical body in the chosen posture.

Be aware of the weight and solidity of the physical structure.

Recall your position within the room and know that you have been practising prana vidya.

Check that the senses are operating normally; sense of smell, taste, hearing and feeling.

If necessary repeat the process of returning the prana to mooladhara.

Do this for several rounds and once more check the senses.

Once the senses are functioning normally, slowly move and stretch the body.

When ready, slowly open the eyes.

The practice is now complete.

Hari Om Tat Sat

PRACTICE 4: AWAKENING PRANA FOR HEALING

Stage 1: Preparation

Assume a comfortable meditation posture.

Practise *kaya sthairyam*, body stillness, for five minutes or so.

Then move inside the body and begin to develop unified awareness of the whole body space as if you are totally empty; nothing inside but space, the only physical part of you is the organ of skin, otherwise, you are hollow like a rubber balloon.

Intensify this feeling of inner space.

Stage 2: Visualizing prana and apana

Within the inner space become aware of prana, the upward movement of energy that occupies the region between the throat and the diaphragm.

Focus on the awareness of this pranic field for some time.

Now become aware of apana.

Apana flows down from the navel to the perineum.

Maintain the awareness with apana.

Now be aware of both prana and apana.

Notice that prana and apana move in opposite directions.

Become physically aware of the natural flow of prana and apana moving in opposite directions.

Go on for some time developing the awareness and experience of prana flowing in this way.

Allow yourself time to become established in the rhythm and movement of prana and apana.

Stage 3: Merging prana and apana at manipura

Now bring in the component of the breath.

With inhalation visualize apana moving upwards and prana moving downwards.

On the exhalation the flows are reversed.

As you exhale, visualize prana and apana meeting at the navel centre, manipura chakra.

Experience this for some time, prana and apana moving away from each other on the inhalation and merging at manipura on the exhalation.

Count up to 27 breaths in this way.

Stage 4: Pingala nadi

Now release the visualization of prana and apana and visualize pingala nadi.

See the chakras, the concentrated centres of energy, shining like jewels along the curving passageway of pingala.

Intensify this awareness and begin to move the breath and awareness up and down pingala nadi.

On inhalation, the breath and awareness ascend, and on the exhalation, the breath and awareness descend.

Continue for some time, allowing your breath and consciousness to curve up and down the pranic passage.

Stage 5: Raising prana

Prepare now to raise prana from mooladhara to ajna.

Inhale, visualize and experience streaks of light spiralling up through pingala while synchronizing the breath with ascending awareness.

Pause at the end of the inhalation, and visualize the light of prana being stored at ajna.

On exhalation, return only the awareness to mooladhara via sushumna.

Go on like this, raising the awakened prana to ajna.

Once sufficient energy has accumulated, maintain the awareness at ajna.

Stage 6: Deepening experience of pranamaya kosha

View ajna as the storehouse of glowing prana in the form of light streaks.

These streaks of light are moving like a myriad of shooting stars or the tail of a comet.

As you concentrate intensely at ajna, visualize eruptions of light or streaks of light particles shooting forth from ajna with lightning velocity.

Intensify this awareness.
At the time of inhalation and distribution, experience streams of white light emanating from ajna throughout the head.
See this light streaming back to ajna at the time of exhalation and withdrawal.
This is direct experience of prana.
Become aware of the whole body.
As you inhale, visualize white light radiating from ajna and pervading the whole body, then withdrawing back to ajna as you exhale.
As you inhale, develop complete awareness of the fluid movement of pranic energy pervading every cell, tissue and organ as it radiates outwards from ajna and illumines the whole body inside and out.
Be aware that this body of light pervades your physical body, but is quite distinct from it.
This subtle, powerful sheath or body of energy is called the *pranamaya kosha*, the body composed of prana.
It puts life in your physical body, but extends beyond it and is experienced in a different dimension.
Experience the white light withdrawing back to ajna with every exhalation then expanding out, again and again, with every inhalation.

Stage 7: Distribution of prana

Saturate the weak, painful or damaged part of the body with prana.
The sensation is similar to that of immersing the part in warm water and experiencing the warmth soaking right through to every molecule.
Take the prana again and again within each cell and tissue of that part.
Inundate it with light energy that you visualize streaming out directly from ajna.
Intensify the practice, using the technique of expansion and contraction.
Withdraw and distribute 27 times or until you feel the

healing dose of prana is sufficient for this session.

In the case of a widespread disorder, you can saturate any parts showing symptoms during the first 27 rounds and then to the whole body 27 times.

In order for the practice to be effective, concentrate on the target intensely, visualizing the part or parts to be healed as clearly as possible.

Stage 8: Returning prana to mooladhara

To end the practice, bring the awareness to ajna and slowly and carefully return all the pranic energies to that chakra.

Become aware of your ujjayi breathing.

Inhale and retain the breath with your concentration at ajna for a few seconds.

Exhale and take the breath and awareness back down sushumna nadi to mooladhara, returning the prana to mooladhara.

Inhale and bring the breath and awareness up pingala, but just the awareness, do not carry any prana with it.

Exhale and take the breath, awareness and prana from ajna to mooladhara via sushumna.

Continue until all the prana has been returned to mooladhara.

Stage 9: Ending the practice

At this point the body should feel very light, the consciousness should be intact and the understanding present.

Release khechari mudra and the ujjayi pranayama; return to normal breathing.

Gradually externalize your awareness.

Be aware of the physical body, its shape and form, and its position within the room.

Check the senses; the sensation of the floor beneath the body, the clothing on the skin, the air on the face.

Be aware of the sense of smell, of taste.

Be aware of sounds, sounds within the room, and sounds from outside.

Ensure that you are in possession of your normal faculties and have complete awareness of your external surroundings.
Stretch the body, move the head from side to side.
The practice is now complete.
If you feel slightly unbalanced, repeat the practice of bringing prana from ajna to mooladhara a few times before again externalizing your awareness in the prescribed manner.
When you are ready, slowly sit up and open your eyes.

Hari Om Tat Sat

PRACTICE 5: AWAKENING PRANA FOR HEALING (VARIATION)

Stage 1: Preparation

Assume a comfortable meditation posture or lie in shavasana.
Practise *kaya sthairyam*, body stillness, for five minutes or so.
Commence ujjayi pranayama and khechari mudra and allow the quality of stillness to deepen.
Complete stillness and steadiness of body and mind.
Shift the awareness to the inner space, the space within the structure of the physical body.
Intensify this feeling of inner space.

Stage 2: Pingala nadi

Now, visualize the silvery-white sushumna passage and the shining chakra jewels.
Bring the weaving, luminous pingala nadi clearly before the mind's eye, criss-crossing from mooladhara up to ajna chakra.
Move your awareness up and down pingala nadi.
Visualize and experience streaks of light spiralling up through pingala while synchronizing the breath with ascending and descending awareness.

Continue, allowing your breath and consciousness to curve gently up and down the pranic passage.

Stage 3: Awakening and raising prana via pingala

Now, leave pingala and visualize ida nadi curving in the opposite direction to pingala.

Then see both passages together.

With inhalation and consciousness of pranic movement, direct your awareness and prana up pingala nadi to ajna.

Hold the awareness for a few seconds at ajna and see the prana glowing brightly.

Then bring only the awareness back down through ida to mooladhara as you exhale.

Continue for several minutes, watching the prana glowing brighter and brighter at ajna chakra as it accumulates.

Continue in this way for a maximum of 27 rounds.

Stage 4: Awakening and raising prana via sushumna

Now focus your attention at sushumna.

Visualize and feel the ascent of pranic energy moving like white light between mooladhara and ajna through the sushumna nadi.

With the breath direct this pranic stream up via sushumna nadi, from mooladhara to ajna.

At ajna, hold the breath for a few seconds with complete, unbroken concentration.

Leave the prana at ajna and return only the breath to mooladhara via sushumna.

Continue in this way for a maximum of 27 rounds.

Stage 5: Distribution of prana

Focus the awareness for a few moments at ajna.

See this storehouse of prana in the form of glowing white light.

As you inhale, visualize streaks of light radiating from ajna and pervading the whole body, then withdrawing back to ajna as you exhale.

As you inhale, prana pervades every single cell of the body.

Experience the white light withdrawing back to ajna with every exhalation then expanding out, again and again, with every inhalation.

Once established in the rhythm of distribution, begin to send prana to the specific areas of the body that require healing.

With the inhalation, flood that part of the body with healing energy, saturating it with warmth and light.

On exhalation, withdraw the energy back to ajna.

Intensify the practice, using the technique of expansion and contraction.

In the case of widespread disorders affecting specific systems of the body, such as the nervous or circulatory systems, send prana to the affected parts first and then to the whole body.

Continue until you know the healing dose of prana to the affected area is sufficient for this session, or for 27 rounds.

Stage 6: Returning prana to mooladhara

To end the practice, bring the awareness to ajna and slowly and carefully return all the pranic energies back to that chakra.

Become aware of your continuous ujjayi breathing.

Inhale and hold the breath with your concentration at ajna for a few seconds.

Exhale and take the awareness back down sushumna nadi to mooladhara, returning the prana to mooladhara.

Inhale and bring the awareness up pingala, but just the breath and awareness, do not carry any prana with it.

Exhale and return the breath, awareness and prana from ajna to mooladhara via sushumna.

Continue until all the prana has been returned to mooladhara.

Stage 7: Ending the practice

Once all the prana has been returned to mooladhara, release khechari and ujjayi pranayama; become aware of the natural breath moving with the body.

Be aware of both the inhalation and the exhalation.
Notice the breath moving parts of the body: the abdomen, the chest, parts of the back.
Feel the whole physical body in the chosen posture.
Be aware of the contact points of the body with the floor.
Feel the sensation of touch this creates.
Notice the feeling of air on the face, the clothing on the skin.
Notice any smells surrounding the body, any taste in the mouth.
Become aware of the space surrounding the body, the space of the room.
Recall the details of the room in your mind's eye and your position within the room.
Be aware of sounds coming from the external environment, near and distant sounds.
Allow the awareness to externalize completely.
Recall the time of day and know the practice is now complete.
Check that all the senses are in functioning normally.
If not, become aware once more of ajna and complete three more rounds of returning the prana to mooladhara and on completion, check the senses in the same way.
Once satisfied that the awareness is completely externalized, begin to make small movements starting with the fingers and toes, and then gradually extend the movements to the whole body.
If in shavasana, keep the eyes closed and come into a sitting position.
Practise palming and gently open the eyes.

Hari Om Tat Sat

16

Healing Others

Practice 1: Self-purification
Practice 2: Healing using a mental image
Practice 3: Healing using a photograph
Practice 4: Healing using an object
Practice 5: Healing by touch – whole body
Practice 6: Healing by touch – specific disorders

This chapter offers a variety of techniques for healing others and includes distance healing. The basic stages of the healing practices are consistent:

1. Settling the body
2. Visualizing a protective yantra
3. Raising and storing prana in ajna
4. Transmitting prana from ajna in the form of healing light, and to end the healing
5. Withdrawing prana and returning it firstly to ajna and finally to mooladhara.

PRACTICE 1: SELF-PURIFICATION

Stage 1: Preparation

Sit in a comfortable meditative posture, preferably siddhasana, siddha yoni asana or padmasana.
Practise kaya sthairyam for five minutes or so.
Commence ujjayi pranayama and khechari mudra.

Stage 2: Awakening and raising prana

Now, become aware of the inner body space.

Visualize the spinal passage and the chakras along this passage.

Develop an intense awareness of pingala nadi.

Then synchronize the ujjayi breath with awareness of pingala.

As you breathe in, the prana rises from mooladhara to ajna along pingala, and as you breathe out, only the breath and awareness descend straight down sushumna from ajna to mooladhara.

Experience the movement of prana moving upward along pingala on inhalation; visualize it as a rapid stream of brilliant light.

Retain the breath at ajna for five seconds repeating mentally, 'ajna, ajna, ajna, ajna, ajna'.Then, while exhaling, bring the breath and awareness back down to mooladhara through sushumna nadi.

Inhale and move the prana with your breath and awareness along pingala nadi from mooladhara to ajna.

Continue awakening the prana along pingala nadi with absolute concentration, feeling the energy movement intensely.

Proceed with this practice until the actual awakening of prana is experienced.

Stage 3: Deepening awareness of pranamaya kosha

Now view ajna as the storehouse of infinite light streaks.

These streaks of light are moving like fireworks or a sparkler.

As you concentrate intensely at ajna, visualize eruptions of light or streaks of light like a myriad of shooting stars or the tail of a comet.

Intensify this awareness.

Become aware of the whole body.

As you inhale, visualize white light radiating from ajna and pervading the whole body, then withdrawing to ajna as you exhale.

At the time of distribution, experience light particles shooting forth from ajna with lightning velocity.
See this light streaming back to ajna at the time of withdrawal.
This is direct experience of prana.
As you inhale, develop complete awareness of the fluid movement of pranic energy pervading every cell, tissue and organ as it emanates from ajna and illumines the body inside, and even for some distance beyond the skin in an aura of light.
Be aware that this body of light pervades your physical body, but is quite distinct from it.
This subtle, powerful sheath or body of energy is *pranamaya kosha*, the body composed of prana.
It is the life force in your physical body, yet extends beyond it and is experienced in a different dimension.
Prana is distributed throughout the whole body on the inhalation and purifies the cells of the body.
Experience the white light withdrawing back to ajna with every exhalation then exploding out through the body, again and again, with every inhalation.
Feel that the whole body is being saturated with prana and that any illness or disease is released into the white light of prana.

Stage 4: Returning prana to mooladhara

When you feel yourself to be totally cleansed, end the practice firstly by returning the prana to ajna.
Bring the awareness to ajna once more, then slowly and carefully begin to return the pranic energies back to mooladhara chakra.
Become aware of your ongoing ujjayi breath.
Inhale and retain the breath with your concentration at ajna for a few seconds.
Exhale and take the breath, awareness and prana back down sushumna nadi to mooladhara, returning the prana to its original source.

Inhale and bring breath and awareness up pingala, but do not carry any prana with it.

Exhale and return breath, awareness and the remaining prana from ajna to mooladhara via sushumna.

Continue until all the prana has been returned to mooladhara.

Stage 5: Ending the practice

To end the practice, release khechari mudra and ujjayi pranayama.

Shift the awareness to the natural breath.

Focus on the breath at the nostrils and be aware of the sensation of the breath there.

Feel the coolness of the breath entering and warmth as the breath exits.

Tune in to the rhythm and sensation of the breath.

Be aware now of the flow of the breath and the movement this creates in the abdomen and chest.

Connect once more to the whole physical body in the chosen posture, its position within the room and all the details of the room you are in.

Become aware of the senses; the sense of touch, of taste, of smell and of hearing.

Be aware of all the sounds in the environment.

Ensure that you are in full possession of your faculties.

Gradually externalize your awareness.

When you feel fully grounded, slowly open your eyes.

If you feel at all unbalanced, close your eyes and repeat the practice of returning prana from ajna to mooladhara a few more times before again externalizing your awareness in the prescribed manner.

When you are ready, slowly begin to move the body and open the eyes.

Hari Om Tat Sat

Practice note: This self-purification may be incorporated at the end of any healing practice.

PRACTICE 2: HEALING USING A MENTAL IMAGE

Stage 1: Preparation

Sit in a comfortable meditative pose, preferably siddhasana, siddha yoni asana or padmasana.

The head and spine should be straight, hands on the knees in chin or jnana mudra.

Commence ujjayi breathing and khechari mudra.

Practise kaya sthairyam for 5–10 minutes making sure the body is totally relaxed and completely still.

Visualize your chosen symbol, either a triangle, cross or circle.

This protective and supportive yantra surrounds the body.

Stage 2: Creating the image

Bring your awareness to ajna chakra and focus it there for a few minutes.

Then visualize the person you wish to help as clearly as possible and meditate upon him or her for a short time.

Stage 3: Spontaneous prana visualization

Hold a distinct image of the person at ajna.

Simultaneously and quickly experience the five pranas within your own body: vyana pervading the whole body; udana spiralling down the legs, arms and up the head; samana travelling side-to-side in the abdomen; apana moving downward between the navel and perineum; and prana moving upward between the diaphragm and throat.

Stage 4: Pingala/sushumna rotation

Retaining the image of the person at ajna, leave the awareness of the pranas and visualize the silvery-white sushumna nadi with ida and pingala criss-crossing each other on either side.

Inhale with ujjayi and direct your breath, awareness and the pranic light up pingala nadi to ajna.

Bring only the breath and awareness back down through sushumna with the exhalation.

At the end of each inhalation, retain the breath and awareness at ajna; see the prana glowing brighter and brighter each time.
Be totally alert and maintain unbroken awareness throughout this practice.
Practise a maximum of 49 rounds.

Stage 5: Transmitting prana to the image

Now focus your awareness on the mental image of the person to be healed.
As you breathe in with ujjayi, visualize shafts of light emanating from ajna and penetrating the whole body of the image.
Then, with exhalation, the prana contracts back to the storehouse at ajna.
With each successive contraction, the emissions of prana become more powerful.
Now focus your awareness on the part to be healed.
Completely saturate the sick or damaged part of the visualized person with healing pranic light.
Send the prana out again and again so that it penetrates each and every cell and tissue of the part being healed.
Inundate it with light energy which you visualize streaming out directly from ajna.
Intensify the practice using the technique of expansion and contraction.
Withdraw and distribute up to 27 times or until you know intuitively that the healing dose of prana is sufficient for this session.
Allow the image of the person to fade.

Stage 6: Returning prana to mooladhara

To end the practice, bring the awareness to ajna once more, then slowly and carefully begin to withdraw the pranic energies back to ajna.
Let go of the symbol and become aware of the body and the breath moving inside.
Become aware of the ongoing ujjayi breathing.

Inhale and retain the breath with your concentration at ajna for a few seconds.

Exhale and take the breath, awareness and prana back down sushumna nadi to mooladhara, returning the prana to its original source.

Inhale and bring breath and awareness up pingala, but just breath and awareness; do not carry any prana with it.

Exhale and return the breath, awareness and the remaining prana from ajna to mooladhara via sushumna.

Continue until all the prana has been returned to mooladhara.

Stage 7: Ending the practice

Release ujjayi and khechari mudra and return to normal breathing.

Become aware of the physical body.

Be aware of the placement of the body in the chosen posture; the arms, legs, head, neck and trunk.

Be aware of the solidity of the body and the shape it creates.

Feel the support of the floor or chair beneath the body.

Be aware of the space surrounding the body and remember the room and your position within it.

Listen to any sounds in the environment and allow the awareness to externalize completely.

Bring the awareness back fully into the body.

When you feel fully grounded slowly open your eyes.

If you feel at all unbalanced, close your eyes and repeat the practice of returning prana from ajna to mooladhara a few more times using ujjayi, before again externalizing your awareness in the prescribed manner.

Hari Om Tat Sat

Practice note: If it is too difficult to maintain the mental image throughout the practice, you can let it fade after the initial visualization and recall it at the time of distributing the prana. In the case of widespread disorders affecting more than one system of the body, prana should be transmitted to the whole body 27 times more after distributing prana to the affected part or parts the initial 27 times., Intense and unbroken concentration on the image of the person to be helped is necessary for healing to take place.

PRACTICE 3: HEALING USING A PHOTOGRAPH

Practice note: For this practice, it is helpful if you can use a photo that contains the part or parts of the body affected by the illness.

Stage 1: Preparation and trataka

Assume a comfortable meditative asana.

Place a photograph of the person to be healed an arm's length away from you with the eyebrow centre at the same level as your own.

Place your hands on your knees in chin or jnana mudra.

Practise kaya sthairyam for five to ten minutes making sure the body is totally relaxed and completely still.

Mentally draw around yourself a protective circle, triangle, cross or your own symbol.

Make it glow with energy.

Let it remain, but let go of it mentally.

Now, open your eyes and perform trataka on the photograph, gazing at the person's eyebrow centre, ideally without blinking, for a minimum of ten minutes.

Stage 2: Visualizing the five pranas

Now start to see clearly and feel vyana darting rapidly in lightning streaks throughout your body.

Leave this visualization and next, visualize udana spiralling down the legs and arms and up the head.

Leave this visualization and experience samana as waves of electric current travelling side-to-side, across the area between the diaphragm and navel.

Leave this visualization and become aware of apana, the downward moving light waves between the navel and the perineum.

Leave this visualization and lastly, concentrate on prana, the upward moving light waves from the diaphragm to the throat.

Be aware of the energy gently building in the body.

Stage 3: Pingala/sushumna rotation

Leave the awareness of the pranas and refresh your awareness of the person's image at ajna.

Bring to the mind's eye the luminous sushumna nadi with ida and pingala on either side, criss-crossing each other in the middle.

Focus the awareness on pingala nadi and commence ujjayi pranayama and khechari mudra.

With the next inhalation, direct your awareness and the pranic light up pingala nadi to ajna.

Retain the breath for a few moments and allow the prana to build at ajna.

On the exhalation, return only the breath and awareness back down through sushumna to mooladhara.

Continue in this way increasing the storehouse of prana at ajna.

See the prana glowing brighter and brighter with every inhalation until ajna is full of energy or for a maximum of 49 rounds of practice.

Stage 4: Transmitting prana to the photographed image

Again, perform trataka on the photograph. This time, focus your full attention for some time on the relevant part of the person to be healed.

Then, as you breathe in with ujjayi and khechari, visualize streaks of light emanating from ajna chakra and penetrating the image.

With exhalation, the prana contracts back to the storehouse at ajna.

Keep performing trataka on the photograph; maintain steady and unbroken concentration.

Keep sending out the prana so that it penetrates every atom of the part or person being healed.

Intensify the practice using the technique of expansion and contraction.

After some time you may notice that the photograph is surrounded by a blue healing light or glow.

Withdraw and distribute prana up to 27 times.

Once complete, close the eyes and allow the afterimage of the photograph to fade from chidakasha.

Stage 5: Returning prana to mooladhara

To end the practice, bring the awareness to ajna once more.

Check that you are aware, then slowly and carefully begin to withdraw the pranic energies back to ajna.

Become aware of your physical body and the ongoing ujjayi breath.

Feel yourself back inside the body.

Let the protective yantra fade.

Inhale and retain the breath with your concentration at ajna for a few seconds.

Exhale and take the breath, awareness and prana back down sushumna nadi to mooladhara, returning the prana to its original source.

Inhale and bring the breath and awareness up pingala; do not carry any prana with it.

Exhale and return the breath, awareness and the remaining prana from ajna to mooladhara via sushumna.

Continue until all the prana has been returned to mooladhara.

Stage 6: Ending the practice

Prepare to end the practice.

Release khechari mudra and ujjayi pranayama.

Shift the awareness to the physical body.

Be aware of all the sensations within the body.

Be aware of the movement of the breath, the different parts of the body touching each other, the floor or chair beneath the body.

Be aware of the whole body in the chosen posture.

Feel the weight and solidity of the body.
Allow the breath to deepen and feel the movement of the body with the breath.
Externalize the awareness and notice sounds in the environment.
Check the other senses; the sense of taste and smell.
Once you feel grounded and senses intact, slowly move the body and gently open the eyes.
If you feel at all unbalanced, before again externalizing your awareness, close your eyes and repeat the practice a few more times, returning prana to mooladhara until the physical body feels completely grounded and the senses are functioning normally.

Hari Om Tat Sat

PRACTICE 4: HEALING USING AN OBJECT

Stage 1: Preparation

Take an object or piece of clothing that the sick person has used or worn recently, preferably something they have frequent contact with.
If it is a piece of clothing, it should be unwashed.
Ensure there are no draughts in the room.
Light a candle and place it on the north side of the object.
Place some burning incense on the east side and a cup of water on the west side.
Then sit down on the south side, facing the candle, in a comfortable meditation posture, preferably siddhasana, siddha yoni asana or padmasana.
Place the left hand on the left knee.
With the right hand hold or touch the object.
Practise kaya sthairyam for five to ten minutes or until the body and mind become steady, calm and peaceful.
Draw around yourself the luminous circle, triangle, cross, or other protective symbol of your choice.

The right hand should maintain contact with the object throughout the practice.

Stage 2: Visualizing the five pranas

Commence ujjayi pranayama and fold the tongue into khechari mudra.

Follow the sound of ujjayi pranayama and become sensitized to the movement of prana within the pranic body.

Now begin to visualize and experience the pancha pranas.

Be aware of the location and distinct movement of each of the five pranas progressively.

Experience vyana . . . udana . . . samana . . . apana . . . prana . . .

Stage 3: Pingala nadi

Release this experience and visualize the curving pathway of pingala nadi weaving through sushumna.

Begin to trace the path of pingala nadi with the awareness.

Move the awareness up and down pingala nadi in rhythm with the ujjayi breath.

Deepen the experience of pingala and visual prana as streams of light flowing with the breath.

The breath, awareness and prana move up and down the psychic passage.

On the next inhalation, begin to raise the prana from mooladhara to ajna.

At ajna, retain the breath for a few seconds, allowing prana to be deposited at ajna.

Return only the breath and awareness to mooladhara.

Go on for some time raising prana in this manner.

Once adequate prana has been awakened and raised, maintain the awareness at ajna for a few moments and experience the bright light of prana stored there.

Stage 4: Flooding the object with prana

Still keeping the eyes closed, focus your full attention on the cloth or object and with the next ujjayi inhalation, send the prana from ajna through the right arm and hand into the object.

As you breathe out with ujjayi, bring your awareness from the object up through the right hand and arm to ajna.

Then again inhale, sending prana through the right arm into the object, and visualize it being saturated with rays of pure, white light streaming down from ajna chakra.

When you exhale, once more bring only your breath and awareness back to ajna; the prana remains in the object.

Perform up to 49 rounds or breaths, visualizing the object glowing brighter and brighter as it becomes infused with prana.

Stage 5: Short meditation

When you have completed up to 49 rounds, remain sitting quietly, still holding the object, and meditate for a minimum of ten minutes on the health of the person you wish to help.

Mentally repeat your guru mantra at this time or, if you do not have one, the Mahamrityunjaya mantra.

Stage 6: Returning prana to mooladhara

To end the practice, bring the awareness to ajna once more.

Slowly and carefully begin to withdraw the pranic energies to that chakra.

Become aware of the physical body inside the protective symbol.

Allow the protective symbol to fade.

Become aware of the body.

Become aware of your ongoing ujjayi breath.

Inhale and retain the breath with your concentration at ajna for a few seconds.

Exhale and take the breath, awareness and prana back down sushumna nadi to mooladhara returning the prana to its original source.

Inhale and bring the breath and awareness up pingala, without carrying any prana with it.

Exhale and return the breath, awareness and the remaining prana from ajna to mooladhara via sushumna.
Continue until all the prana has been returned to mooladhara.

Stage 7: Ending the practice

Once the prana has been returned to its source, shift the awareness to the body and the breath.
Release khechari mudra and ujjayi pranayama.
Be aware of the natural process of breathing and the stillness and steadiness of the body in the chosen posture.
Be aware of the whole body from head to toe.
Be aware of the form and structure of the physical body.
Extend the awareness outwards and visualize the room in which you are sitting.
Be aware of sounds in the environment, inside and outside the room.
Check the other senses systematically; notice any smells or odours, any taste in the mouth, feel the touch of clothing on the skin and air on the face.
Ensure that you are in full possession of your faculties, that all the senses are intact, and gradually externalize your awareness.
Bring the awareness back into the body.
The practice is now complete.
If you wish, practise palming, then slowly open your eyes.

Hari Om Tat Sat

PRACTICE 5: HEALING BY TOUCH – WHOLE BODY

Practice note: A short yoga nidra may be given before or after to supplement healing. The visualization may include seeing their whole body glowing with perfect health and vitality. However, this may not be appropriate for every person and thus discrimination must be applied carefully.

Stage 1: Preparation

The person to be healed should lie in shavasana and be prepared as for yoga nidra so they are mentally and physically relaxed.

Sit behind their head, preferably in siddhasana, siddha yoni asana or padmasana. Visualize a luminous circle, triangle, cross, or other symbol of your choice surround your physical body. See your physical body within this protective yantra.

Now place the palms of your hands on the temples of the person with your fingers gently touching the cheeks and jawbone.

While the person relaxes and watches the breath, you have to go through the following stages 2 to 4.

Stage 2: Visualizing the five pranas

Commence ujjayi breathing and khechari mudra.

Focus on the soft, subtle sound of the psychic breath.

Allow ujjayi to refine the awareness and tune in to the pranic body.

Become aware of vyana . . . udana . . . samana . . . apana . . . prana . . .

Stage 3: Pingala nadi

Leave the five pranas and visualize ida and pingala crisscrossing through sushumna nadi.

See the chakras, studded along the sushumna nadi, radiating energy and light.

Concentrate the awareness at pingala and begin to move the awareness up and down pingala.

Synchronize the ascent and descent with the inhalation and exhalation.

Be aware of ujjayi, the subtle psychic breath.
Establish a rhythm, the breath and awareness united.

Stage 4: Building prana at ajna

Prepare to raise prana through pingala using the breath and concentrated awareness.
With inhalation and consciousness of pranic movement, direct your awareness up pingala nadi to ajna.
Retain the breath, awareness and prana for a few seconds at ajna and see the prana glowing brightly.
Then bring only the breath and awareness back down to mooladhara as you exhale.
Continue for several minutes, watching the prana glowing brighter and brighter at ajna chakra as it accumulates.

Stage 5: Cleansing the pranic body

When you are sure you have awakened your prana, open your eyes and kneel or stand beside your patient.
Begin to make downward sweeping passes with the hands held at a distance of about three inches from the body, palms facing downwards.
This movement goes right down from the head to the feet and should be performed eleven times.

Stage 6: Treating general disorders or illnesses of the body

Position yourself on the right side of the patient's body at about the waist.
After making the sweeping passes, place your left hand on the person's forehead, over ajna chakra.
Then place your right hand at the person's manipura chakra, just over the navel.
Hold your awareness at your ajna chakra for a few seconds, with full awareness of the prana stored there.
Inhale and send prana through the left hand with ujjayi and khechari, and see the brilliant light stored at your ajna chakra charging the ajna chakra of the patient.
Simultaneously, send energy streaming through the right hand and see the person's manipura chakra being saturated by white healing light.

Exhale and bring your awareness back to your ajna chakra.

Inhale and distribute prana through both hands, exhale and return the awareness to your ajna chakra.

This should be repeated a maximum of 49 times.

Stage 7: Self-purification

Return the awareness to your ajna chakra and rest there for a few breaths.

Be aware of your own guru or the source of light within you.

Let go of any feeling of doership and connect with the inner source.

Be aware that a body of vital energy pervades your physical body, yet is quite distinct from it.

This subtle, powerful sheath or body of energy is *pranamaya kosha*, the body composed of prana.

It puts life in your physical body; however it extends beyond it and is experienced in a different dimension.

Feel that your whole body is composed of prana and any weakness or illness is dispersed by the white light of prana.

Stage 8: Returning prana to mooladhara

When you feel yourself to be totally cleansed, end the practice by returning the prana.

Bring the awareness to ajna once more, then slowly and carefully begin to withdraw the pranic energies to that chakra.

When you have finished withdrawing the prana to ajna, withdraw your hands from the person.

Be aware again of the protective symbol surrounding your physical body and allow it to fade.

Become aware of the body and the ujjayi breathing.

Inhale and retain the breath with your concentration at ajna for a few seconds.

Exhale and take the breath, awareness and prana back down sushumna nadi to mooladhara, returning the prana to its original source.

Inhale and bring only the breath and awareness up pingala leaving the prana at mooladhara.
Exhale and return the breath, awareness and the remaining prana from ajna to mooladhara via sushumna.
Continue until all the prana has been returned to mooladhara.

Stage 9: Ending the practice

Once all the prana has been returned to its source, release khechari mudra and the ujjayi breathing.
Become aware of the natural breath.
Focus on the natural ingoing and outgoing breath.
Notice the rhythm and flow of the breath within the physical body.
Be aware now of the whole body and its position.
Be aware of the placement of the limbs, the head, neck and trunk.
Feel the floor beneath the body and become aware of the surroundings.
Be aware of all the senses; sense of touch, taste, smell, and hearing.
Ensure that you are in full possession of your faculties and that the senses are all operating normally.
Check that the awareness is fully externalized.
When you feel fully grounded, slowly open your eyes.
If you feel at all unbalanced, close your eyes and repeat the practice of returning prana from ajna to mooladhara three more times before again externalizing your awareness in the prescribed manner.

Hari Om Tat Sat

Practice note: After you have withdrawn your hands from the person you are healing, they should continue to lie in shavasana with eyes closed. When you are fully externalized yourself, guide the person to externalize their awareness.

PRACTICE 6: HEALING BY TOUCH – SPECIFIC DISORDERS

Practice note: The following variation for stage 6 can supplement or substitute the general healing outlined in the previous practice (Practice 5). In that practice, prana was distributed to the ajna and manipura chakras of the patient in order to heal the whole body. The following technique heals specific areas of the body in order to facilitate healing.

Stage 6: Treating localized disorders

After making the cleansing, sweeping passes, place the right hand on or just over the specific area to be treated, palm facing downwards.

Focusing your attention there, breathe in with ujjayi while visualizing the white light at your ajna chakra being projected to the affected area through your right arm and hand.

Exhale and let the awareness return to ajna but leave the prana in the area being treated.

Perform up to 49 rounds or breaths, visualizing that part of the person's body glowing with pranic light.

17

Advanced Prana Vidya with the Masters

PRACTICE 1: PRANA VIDYA WITH SWAMI SATYANANDA SARASWATI (INTERNAL DISTRIBUTION)

Stage 1: Preparation

Close your eyes as gently as possible and get ready to practise prana vidya.

In order to avoid distractions, it is very important that the eyes should remain closed.

You may sit in any comfortable pose, in an easy chair or even recline on your bed, but please remember that your position should not cause any discomfort.

Stage 2: Awakening prana

As far as the awakening of prana is concerned, remember distinctly the spiral movement of prana (along pingala nadi) from mooladhara to ajna.

Start from the right side and then proceed carefully, keeping pace with your breath.

From mooladhara turn to the right, make a curve and reach swadhisthana.

Move upwards to manipura along the left side curve.

From manipura to anahata rise along the right curve.

From anahata to vishuddhi ascend along the left curve.

From vishuddhi to ajna follow the curve along the right.

Thus takes place the spiral movement (along pingala) from mooladhara to ajna, and the awakening of prana.

Continue practising in this way.
In the beginning you have to complete 49 rounds, but when you become used to the practice, then you no longer need to count the number of rounds because you feel the awakening of prana instinctively.
When the awakening of prana has commenced from mooladhara to ajna, and you feel the movement of the pranic force, only then can you commence your further journey.

Stage 3: Raising prana

Start raising the prana from mooladhara to ajna in the same way as you have been practising, but leave the prana at ajna, do not take it back to mooladhara.
Commence your journey with watchful awareness from mooladhara to ajna. Let your mind and consciousness, with psychic and pranic energies, keep on rising in and through the spinal cord.
Go on diligently with your practice.
The kundalini is to be awakened at mooladhara.
Let it rise gradually to ajna, then pause briefly at ajna in the form of kumbhaka.
Here ends our first round, only to step into the second.
Recommence your journey from mooladhara; stop at ajna with a brief kumbhaka.
Continue with absolute concentration, intensely feeling the movement of prana.
Keep on awakening the pranic force along the psychic route (of pingala) from mooladhara to ajna.
When you reach ajna chakra, remember to remain there in kumbhaka for some time.

Stage 4: Expansion and relaxation

After performing kumbhaka at ajna, exhale and relax your whole body.
You are not exhaling through the spinal cord; you are exhaling through the body like a balloon releasing air.
With inhalation the body expands, breathing in through every pore of the skin.

Relaxation comes with every exhalation, and expansion with every inhalation.
The form of breathing will be ujjayi pranayama.
Don't feel it in the spinal cord, but feel it in the body.
Now this ujjayi becomes all-pervading in the body, as if every pore of the body is breathing in ujjayi.
When you inhale, every pore in the body assists you in inhalation and the body expands like a balloon.
When you exhale, your whole body exhales and becomes as light as cotton; it is the time of relaxation.
Total body awareness and synchronization of breath consciousness with body consciousness.
Complete awareness of the whole body.
Now inhale, and with the inhalation the whole body is breathing in through the pores, through the skin, through every part of the body.
Your whole body is expanding with inhalation.
Exhale and with the exhalation every pore of the body is breathing out.
Now the body relaxes.
Remember that the entire process of inhalation and exhalation takes place through ajna chakra behind the centre of the eyebrows.
Ajna is the focal point; it is the main distributing agency of the entire respiratory system.
It is from ajna chakra that the inhaled prana proceeds to the entire body; the prana to be exhaled first returns to ajna chakra, and from ajna the exhaled prana is expelled.
During inhalation there is expansion of the body.
During exhalation there is relaxation of the body.
When you inhale from ajna chakra and expand the whole body, feel that it is from ajna chakra, the storehouse of prana, and that prana is being distributed to the entire body.
During exhalation, the prana is withdrawn back to ajna, not through any psychic passage, but directly.

Ujjayi breathing is to be practised in in the following way: From ajna, inhale and distribute the prana throughout the whole body right to the toes.

During exhalation, withdraw the prana back to ajna and relax.

It is natural to relax when you exhale.

This exercise is much easier to follow than the previous one.

In the previous exercise you were breathing in through the pores of the body and also breathing out through the same pores, but here the whole breathing process is to be carried out through the agency of ajna chakra. Ajna chakra may be considered as the storehouse of prana from where prana is distributed to the entire body system with the help of ujjayi breathing. During exhalation, prana is withdrawn from all directions back to ajna chakra.

Remember that relaxation follows exhalation.

During relaxation, both consciousness as well as prana withdraw themselves from the body to ajna.

There is relaxation and not contraction of the body.

You should become so used to ujjayi that during the process of prana vidya your entire consciousness, imagination, feeling, thinking and also your physical system should expand with inhalation and relax with exhalation.

You should become so indifferent to the breathing process that not even a fraction of your consciousness should be aware of it.

The prana is expanding your astral body during inhalation and relaxing your astral body during exhalation.

Your total awareness should be focused on the whole process of expansion and relaxation.

Your centre of gravity should shift from the processes of breathing to the processes of expansion and relaxation.

In short, you must transcend the breathing consciousness.

Stage 5: Expansion and contraction

Now we shall proceed to the next stage, where there is a slight variation.

Here there will be expansion with every round of inhalation as in the previous stage, but during exhalation, instead of relaxation, there will be contraction.

Expand with inhalation, and distribute the prana from ajna chakra to the entire body.

That is, during inhalation prana moves from ajna to various parts of the body and the body expands at the same time.

When you exhale, prana returns to ajna chakra, causing contraction of the astral body.

You can understand the whole exercise if you remember two rules.

On inhalation, there is distribution of prana and expansion of the body.

On exhalation, there is withdrawal of prana and contraction of the body.

The process of expansion and contraction of the body is not physical but mental.

You have to stretch your imagination to its possible limits.

When you direct your prana to any part of the body, for example the foot, then feel mentally as if your foot is expanding in all directions.

It is not physical expansion, but psychic and pranic expansion.

Thus, when you inhale, distribute your prana in all directions, so that prana which has started from ajna extends and covers the entire body.

Your whole body from top to toe is saturated with pranic force.

Feel this intensely.

Simultaneously, you must imagine that your psychic body is expanding extensively in all directions, and it has assumed cosmic form.

Similarly, when you exhale, consciously withdraw your pranas from all parts of the body and direct it to ajna chakra.

Just as water in the ocean recedes when the tidal flow is reversed, so also prana recedes during exhalation, and contraction takes place.

In contraction, body consciousness is transcended.

But remember that contraction and expansion are not to be effected in parts, but as a whole.

The body, as one homogeneous unit, is to be expanded on inhalation and contracted on exhalation as the case may be.

When you inhale, distribute prana from ajna to all parts of the body, and when you exhale bring the expanded pranic force back to the source, ajna.

Stage 6: Distributing prana to individual body parts: expansion/relaxation

This time we will do the exercise in parts.

We shall start with the right arm; inhale and supply the pranic force to the right arm from ajna.

Expand your right arm, not physically but mentally.

Now exhale, withdraw your prana from the right arm back to ajna and relax your right arm.

When you distribute prana to the right arm, feel the prana there permeating every pore of the limb right down to the fingertips.

Feel the movement of prana.

Come back to ajna; retain your breath for a short time.

Go to the left arm; supply prana to the fingertips of the left hand.

Now withdraw the prana back to ajna.

Prana proceeds from ajna to the left arm and returns to ajna from the left arm.

You are expanding and relaxing your arms alternately with every supply and withdrawal of prana.

Come back to ajna; retain the breath there.

Exhale and relax.

Now inhale, and with the inhalation supply prana to the right leg through the right side of the back.
Mentally feel the expansion of your right leg.
Now exhale, withdraw your prana from the right leg back to ajna.
With the withdrawal of prana relax your right leg.
Now supply prana to the left leg, right to the tips of the toes; expansion follows every round of supply.
Withdraw prana from the left leg back to ajna and relax.
Now repeat.
Supply – expand; withdraw – relax.
Supply – expand; withdraw – relax.
Bring your prana back to ajna and listen.
From ajna, supply prana to your right chest, and withdraw the prana back to ajna during exhalation.
Inhale – supply – expand; exhale – withdraw – relax.
Now bring your prana back to ajna and retain the breath.
Inhale, supply prana to your left chest and expand your chest mentally, avoiding the heart muscles.
Exhale, withdraw prana from the left chest, then relax your chest.
Supply – expand; withdraw – relax.

Stage 7: Distributing prana to individual body parts: expansion/contraction

Now come back to ajna, retain the breath and listen to the instructions.
This time during the withdrawal of prana, instead of relaxation you will have to contract.
First of all, supply prana to the right arm and expand.
Withdraw prana from the right arm back to ajna and contract.
Come back to ajna, and maintain awareness of prana in ajna.
Inhale, supply prana to the left arm and expand it.
Exhale, withdraw prana and contract.
Both the processes of expansion and contraction are to be done mentally.

Withdraw your prana back to ajna; retain it in ajna for some time.

Mentally relax your left arm, then go to the right leg.

Supply prana from ajna to the whole right leg, down to the tips of your toes, through the right side of the back, and now expand.

Withdraw prana, exhale, and contract your right leg mentally.

Return to ajna, retain your breath, mentally release your right leg.

Supply prana to the left leg with expansion.

Withdraw prana from the left leg back to ajna with contraction.

Retain the prana in ajna, and mentally release your left leg.

Supply prana to the right side of the chest with expansion, withdraw with contraction, come back to ajna.

Relax the right side of the chest.

Now supply prana to the left side and expand the chest mentally, avoiding the heart.

Withdraw prana with contraction; come back to ajna and retain the prana for some time.

Stage 8: Vision of prana shakti

Now you should have a vision of prana shakti.

Supply the prana directly to the whole of your body.

Then withdraw the prana back to ajna: no contraction, no expansion, no retention.

If they take place on their own, well and good, but don't worry if these processes do not accompany the supply and withdrawal of prana.

The most important thing is to get a vision of light streaks proceeding from ajna to the body during the period of supply.

During withdrawal of prana, shafts of light must withdraw back to ajna.

Just as from a charcoal fire you find little sparks shooting forward with a hissing noise, or you see light streaks shooting forth from fireworks, or during the welding process sparks are seen, in the same manner, where prana is supplied to the various limbs, visualize the pranic energy in the form of light particles issuing from ajna to the part where prana is directed.

Imagine ajna to be the storehouse of infinite light streaks, like a volcanic bed, and as soon as eruption takes place, streaks of light particles issue forth with lightning velocity.

These streaks of light permeate the whole body and when the eruption stops, the energy in the form of light sparks withdraws to the source, only to reappear at the next explosion.

Stage 9: Returning prana to mooladhara

Now withdraw your prana back to ajna.

Inhale and retain the breath, concentrating at ajna.

Exhale and let the prana descend from ajna to mooladhara via sushumna passage.

Continue this practice until you are sure all the prana has been returned to mooladhara.

Then slowly and carefully become aware of your external environment.

Once your awareness is fully externalized, slowly move your body and open your eyes.

Hari Om Tat Sat

PRACTICE 2: PRANA VIDYA WITH SWAMI NIRANJANANANDA SARASWATI (EXTERNAL DISTRIBUTION)

Stage 1: Preparation

In this practice the prana is distributed externally.

It is therefore recommended that you sit comfortably or lie down in shavasana so that you can be still.

Make the body and mind calm and peaceful.

If you are sitting up, make sure your body weight is equally distributed on both sides.

Begin to observe your breathing process.

As you breathe in and out, totally relax the body.

Become perfectly motionless.

Tell yourself mentally, 'I shall not move throughout the duration of the practice. I shall remain aware and alert.'

Remember that you should not break the flow of awareness; there should be no wavering of your concentration.

Stage 2: Awakening prana

Become aware of the inner body space.

Within the space, visualize the spinal passage and the chakras.

Develop an intense awareness of pingala nadi.

Then synchronize the ujjayi breath with awareness of pingala and fold the tongue back into khechari mudra.

As you breathe in, the breath rises from mooladhara to ajna along pingala.

As you breathe out, the breath descends straight down sushumna from ajna to mooladhara.

Experience the movement of prana in pingala nadi.

Visualize it in the form of a rapid stream of light.

Move the prana with your awareness and breathe up along pingala nadi from mooladhara to ajna.

Retain the breath at ajna for five seconds repeating mentally, 'ajna, ajna, ajna, ajna, ajna'.

Then, while exhaling, bring the awareness back down to mooladhara through sushumna nadi, leaving the prana at ajna.

Continue awakening the prana along pingala nadi with absolute concentration, feeling the energy movement intensely.

Continue this practice until the actual awakening of prana is experienced.

In the beginning practise 49 rounds.

When you have mastered the practice, however, you will feel the awakening of prana instinctively.

Stage 3: Distribution of prana

Once you have raised the prana to ajna chakra, concentrate your awareness there and visualize the dynamic, glowing light of the prana you have stored.

Feel the throbbing sensation of this accumulated force.

Then visualize a luminous circle or an upward pointing triangle around your body, or a luminous cross that passes through your body.

Once one of those shapes has been clearly perceived and you can see it shining brightly, begin to stretch the prana outward in one or all directions.

Visualize pranic light expanding outside your physical body.

If you have not yet developed the technique beyond imagination, the experience will be mental only.

However, if you have actually awakened the prana, the streaks of light emanating from the body will be dazzling, clear and sharp.

Now, inhaling with ujjayi, stretch the prana out from ajna chakra using your willpower.

Visualize light energy expanding in all directions, pervading the whole body and then stretching beyond the body.

Then, with the exhalation, withdraw the prana back to the storehouse at ajna and relax.

Visualize the pranic glow increasing as it is concentrated.

As you continue inhaling and exhaling in ujjayi, see the prana stretch out further and further on each inhalation.

First it fills and encompasses the circle, triangle or cross around your body.

Watch this process for some time.
Then see it stretching beyond to fill the room in which you are practising.
See the whole room being saturated with rays of bright light every time you inhale. Then, on the exhalation, this light concentrates back to ajna chakra.
Next, the prana extends still further to encompass the environment around you and the whole neighbourhood.
Go on experiencing this.
With perseverance it will become an actual experience.
Continue developing your awareness of the prana engulfing wider and wider areas; the city, the state, the whole country, and, with each exhalation, draw the prana back to ajna.
See the great pranic force spreading out over the whole continent, saturating everyone and everything in healing light.
There is absolutely no limit to the distance you can stretch this healing power.
Imagine the prana being sent out to encompass the entire world and then the universe.
In this way, merge your prana with universal prana.

Stage 4: Ending the practice

To end the practice, withdraw the prana back to ajna and hold the awareness at that chakra for some time while practising ujjayi pranayama.
Check that you have returned all your prana to ajna.
Become aware of the luminous circle, triangle or cross that you have defined around your physical body.
Visualize your body enveloped by this luminous shape.
When this awareness is quite clear, begin to dissolve the luminous shape.
Again, concentrate at ajna and begin to return the prana to mooladhara via sushumna nadi as you exhale, until all the prana has been returned to its source.
Slowly and carefully come back to normal body consciousness.

Become aware of the physical environment and your sensory perceptions.
Feel the contact of the body against the floor, feel the air on the face, the hands and the feet, be aware of any taste within the mouth and any subtle smells or fragrances that fill the air.
Be aware of the surrounding environment and listen to the sounds coming from all directions.
Allow these sounds to externalize the awareness completely.
Remember the time of day, your position within the room.
The practice is now complete.
Slowly begin to move the body and when you are ready, open the eyes.

Hari Om Tat Sat

Appendices

Appendix A

The Pranic Body

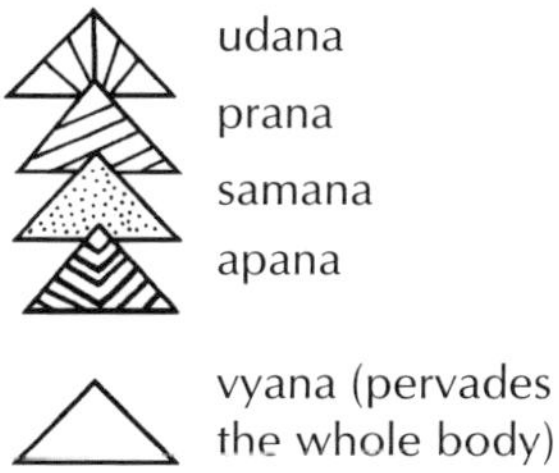

Appendix B

Internal Organs

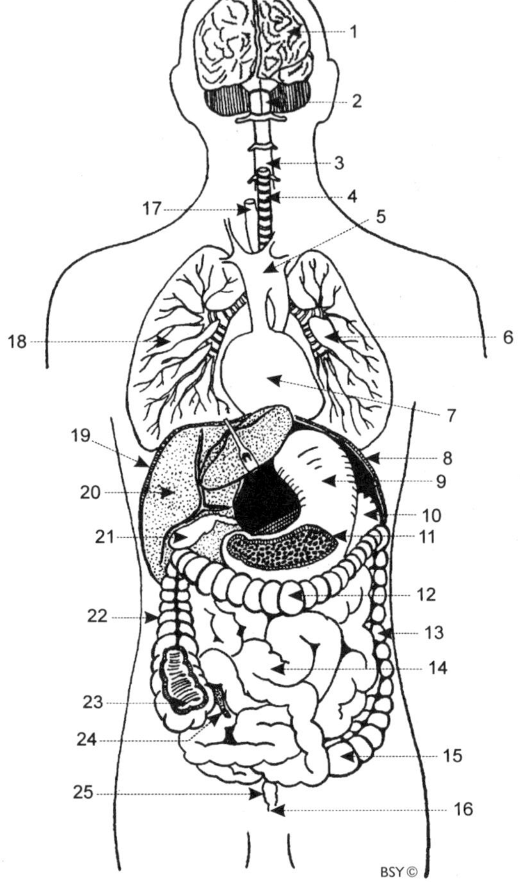

1. Brain
2. Cerebellum
3. Spinal cord
4. Trachea
5. Aorta
6. Left Lung
7. Heart
8. Diaphragm
9. Stomach
10. Spleen
11. Pancreas
12. Transverse colon (large intestine)
13. Descending colon
14. Small intestine
15. Sigmoid colon
16. Anus
17. Oesophagus
18. Right Lung
19. Diaphragm
20. Liver
21. Gall Bladder
22. Ascending colon
23. Cecum
24. Appendix
25. Rectum

Appendix C

Location of Chakras

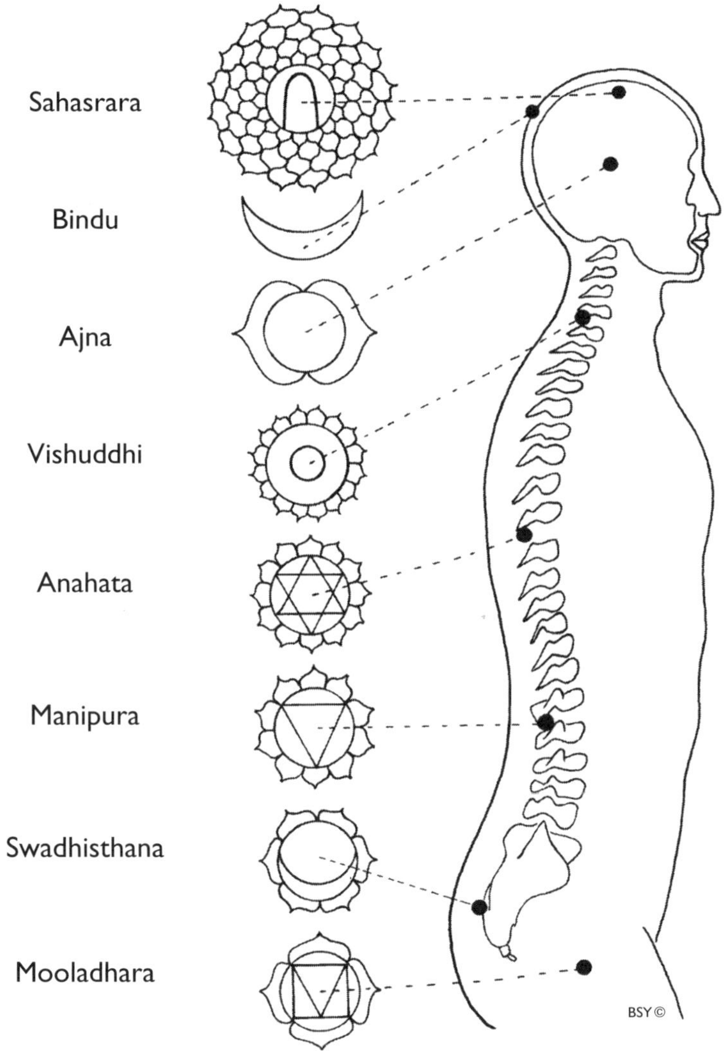

Glossary

Abhisheka – ceremonial bath; consecration

Abhyasa – constant and steady practice without any interruption; to remain established in the effort of sadhana

Achara – conduct; good behaviour; custom; an established rule of conduct

Acharya – one knowing or teaching the acharas or rules; teacher, preceptor, spiritual guide

Agama – historical sacred literature; the philosophy and scriptures of tantra where Lord Shiva teaches his consort Parvati

Ajapa japa – continuous, spontaneous repetition of mantra; meditation practice in which mantra is coordinated with the breath

Ajna chakra – psychic centre situated at the medulla oblongata on the top of the spinal column, corresponding to the pineal gland; seat of intuition; psychic centre where guru's commands are received

Akasha – ether, space

Anahata chakra – psychic centre situated in the region of the cardiac plexus

Anandamaya kosha – sheath or body of bliss

Annamaya kosha – sheath or body of matter; the physical body

Antar – internal

Anushthana – a resolve to perform a mantra sadhana with absolute discipline for a requisite period of time; a fixed course of sadhana

Apana – one of the pancha pranas moving downwards from the navel to the perineum in the lower abdominal region, responsible for elimination and reproduction

Asana – a steady and comfortable meditative pose; third step of ashtanga or raja yoga

Ashram – hermitage, hut, cell, dwelling or abode of asceticism or spiritual practice

Atmabhava – feeling of unity with all; seeing the atman (soul) equally in all beings

Avahana – invocation using mantras so the deity manifests during the time of worship

Bahiranga – external limb or stage

Bhava – feeling, emotion

Bhrumadhya – trigger point for ajna chakra located at the eyebrow centre

Bindu chakra – psychic centre situated at the top of the back of the head; centre or source of individual creation from where psychic vibrations first emanate

Brahmamuhurta – the time between 4 am and 6 am, best suited to spiritual sadhana

Chaitanya – consciousness

Chakra – a psychic/pranic centre in the subtle body; circle, wheel or vortex; congregation point of nadis

Chhandogya Upanishad – name of the Upanishad from the Sama Veda teaching the origin and significance of the mantra *Om*

Chidakasha – inner space visualized in meditation behind the closed eyes or in the region of ajna chakra

Chin mudra – psychic gesture of consciousness

Chitta shakti – mental force

Darshan – a glimpse, seeing, observing; sight, vision; knowing, understanding

Dharana – concentration or complete attention; sixth limb of Sage Patanjali's ashtanga yoga

Dharma – the natural role one plays in life; ethical law; duty; religion

Dhyana – meditation; seventh limb of Sage Patanjali's ashtanga yoga

Drishti – faculty of seeing

Ganga – the river Ganges; the most sacred river in India

Gayatri – a vedic metre of 24 syllables; a most famous and sacred mantra

Granthi – psychic knot; three granthis along sushumna nadi hinder the upward passage of kundalini

Guru – preceptor; one who dispels the darkness caused by *avidya* or ignorance

Hatha yoga – system of yoga for attaining physical and mental purity, and balancing the pranas in the body

Homa – sacrificial fire which symbolizes the divine light on earth; ritualistic process in which oblations are offered into the fire

Hridayakasha – psychic space of the heart centre, experienced between manipura and vishuddhi charkas, associated with anahata chakra

Ida – major nadi beginning on the left side of mooladhara and twisting up the spine through the chakras to ajna, through which manas shakti or lunar energy flows; governing the left side of the body and right side of the brain; associated with internalized awareness

Japa – continuous repetition of mantra

Jnana – true knowledge; wisdom

Jnana mudra – psychic gesture of knowledge

Kaya sthairyam – practice of absolute steadiness and awareness of the physical body often performed as a preparation for pranayama or meditative states

Khechari mudra – tongue lock; a hatha yoga practice in which the elongated tongue passes back into the pharynx to stimulate the flow of life-giving nectar; a milder raja yoga practice where the tongue is inserted in, or folded backwards towards the upper cavity of the palate

Koorma – the minor prana responsible for opening and closing the eyes, blinking, and controlling the movement of the eyelids

Kosha – body or realm of experience or existence; covering of the self which limits manifestation of the ultimate reality

Kriya – action; motion; action leading to perfection of knowledge

Kriya yoga – practices of kundalini yoga designed to speed up the evolution of humanity

Kumbhaka – breath retention

Kundalini shakti – also referred to as 'kundalini'; potential energy lying dormant in mooladhara chakra, often referred to as the 'serpent power'

Kundalini yoga – path of yoga which awakens the dormant spiritual force

Mahaprana – cosmic, universal prana; prana in its cosmic unmanifest aspect

Mahamrityunjaya – a form of Shiva; 'the great one who is victorious over death'

Mahamrityunjaya mantra – mantra that purifies, heals, transforms and brings 'great victory over death'

Mahasamadhi – final liberation experienced by an elevated soul on the departure of the spirit from the body

Manas – finite, rational mind, concerned with senses, thought and counter-thought

Manas shakti – mental or lunar energy

Manipura chakra – psychic and pranic centre situated behind the navel in the spinal column, corresponding to the solar plexus

Manomaya kosha – sheath or body of mental experience

Mantra – subtle sound or combination of sound vibrations revealed to sages in deep meditation, used for liberating consciousness from the limitations of mundane awareness

Moolabandha – contraction of the perineum in the male and cervix in the female body; perineal lock

Mooladhara chakra – lowest psychic and pranic centre in the human body; situated in the perineum in the male and cervix in women; base storehouse of prana shakti

Mouna – silence, measured speech; remaining silent for a specified span of time

Mudra – literally 'gesture'; physical, mental and psychic attitude which expresses and channels cosmic energy

Murti – body, solid part of the body; form, shape, figure, statue, person; symbol; idol

Nada yoga – the yoga of subtle sound

Nadi – flow, subtle channel of energy in the pranic body

Nidra – deep sleep; isolation from mind and the senses; unconscious state; shutting off; sleepiness; one of the five vrittis listed in Sage Patanjali's *Yoga Sutras*

Nirvana – cessation of suffering, final liberation or emancipation in Buddhist thought; higher state of existence or awareness

Niyama – rule; the second limb of ashtanga or raja yoga comprising of five rules of personal discipline or observances of behaviour, viz. *shaucha,* purity; *santosha,* contentment; *tapas,* austerity or penance; *swadhyaya,* self-study and *Ishwara pranidhana,* dedication to the highest principle

Nyasa – practice of assigning the various parts of the body to different deities, which is usually accompanied with mantras and corresponding mudras or gestures

Om – or 'Aum', bija mantra of ajna chakra; the universal cosmic sound representing the four states of consciousness

Ojha – traditional healer

Pancha kosha – the five sheaths, bodies or realms of experience and existence

Pancha prana – five major divisions of pranic energy located in the physical body, viz. apana, prana, samana, udana, vyana

Pancharatra – system of tantra originated from the Vaishnava sect

Paramatma – cosmic soul or consciousness, supreme self; the atma (soul) of the entire universe, of the individual as well as the cosmos; liberated state of the inner self

Patanjali – author of the *Yoga Sutras* and propounder of ashtanga yoga; contemporary of Lord Buddha

Peeth – seat; often used to denote a place of divine power

Pingala nadi – major nadi beginning on the right side of mooladhara and spiralling up the spine through the chakras to ajna, conducting the dynamic prana shakti; governs the right side of the body and left side of the brain; associated with externalized awareness; also called surya nadi

Pooja – worship; honour; respect; rites

Prakriti – cosmic energy; manifest and unmanifest nature; nature or primordial matter

Prana – vital force, essence of life permeating the whole of creation, both the macrocosmos and the microcosmos; one of the pancha pranas which operates between the diaphragm and base of the throat in the region of the heart and lungs, also referred to as 'sthula prana'

Prana nigraha – control of prana

Prana pratishtha – tantric ritual by which an image or symbol of God or any deity is vitalized

Prana shakti – the force of prana; vital or solar energy

Pranamaya kosha – sheath or body of pranic energy

Pranayama – a series of techniques for controlling and expanding the dimension of prana; fourth limb of ashtanga or raja yoga

Pratishtha – reputation; awareness of identity; base, ground, support

Pratyahara – sense withdrawal; fifth limb of ashtanga or raja yoga

Purusha Sukta – a hymn from the *Rigveda* which praises creation and the creator who pervades it

Raja yoga – 'the royal yoga'; yoga of awakening the psychic awareness and faculties through meditation

Rigveda – oldest of the four Vedas and the most ancient sacred book of the Hindus

Rudra granthi – literally 'knot of Rudra'; psychic knot in the vishuddhi and ajna chakras symbolizing attachment to siddhis or higher mental attributes

Sadhaka – one who practises sadhana; spiritual aspirant

Sadhana – spiritual practice or discipline performed regularly for the attainment of inner experience and self-realization

Sahasrara – abode of superconsciousness; highest psychic centre which symbolizes the threshold between the psychic and spiritual realms, located at the crown of the head, associated with the pituitary gland

Samadhi – culmination of meditation; state of unity with the object of meditation and the universal consciousness; final step of raja yoga

Samana – one of the pancha pranas; sideways moving prana situated between the navel and the diaphragm, pranic force of manipura

Samskara – mental impression stored in the subtle body as an archetype

Sanatana dharma – system of eternal values underlying the vedic civilization

Sankalpa – will, volition; positive resolve; purpose, aim, intention; determination, conviction; desire, wish

Sanskrit – original vedic language in which most Indian scriptures are written

Shakti – primal energy; manifest consciousness; subtle creative and vital energy; counterpart of Shiva

Shanti – pacification, peace, calmness, tranquillity, quiet, ease, rest

Shaktipat – higher energy or experience transmitted by the guru to a worthy disciple; descent of power through worship

Shastras – sacred book; department of knowledge; science

Shatkarma – 'six actions'; chiefly, group of six purificatory practices of classical hatha yoga, viz. dhauti, basti, neti, nauli, trataka and kapalbhati

Shavasana – corpse pose; pose of relaxation

Sheshanaga – name of a scriptural serpent said to have one thousand heads, represented as forming the couch on which Vishnu (preserver of the universe) reclines, or as supporting the entire universe on his head

Shiva – 'auspicious one' or 'good'; name of the god of the sacred Hindu trinity who is entrusted with the work of destruction; destroyer of ego and duality; cosmic consciousness, counterpart of Shakti; the first or original yogi

Shivalingam – black oval-shaped stone worshipped as symbol of Shiva; symbol of consciousness

Shodhana – purification

Shoonya – void; state of absolute nothingness

Sri Yantra – geometric symbol representing the divine 'female' energy; designed for concentration or meditation in order to unleash hidden potential within the consciousness

Shuddhi – purification

Siddha – perfected being; accomplished soul particularly characterized by eight supernatural faculties called siddhis

Siddhi – perfection; paranormal or supernormal accomplishment; control of mind and prana

So-Ham – literally 'I am That'; mantra used in ajapa japa; the unconscious repetitive sound produced by the breath, the inhalation sounding 'So' and the exhalation 'Ham'

Sthulakasha – space pervading the physical body

Sthula prana – see prana

Sushumna nadi – main nadi in the centre of the spinal cord through which kundalini shakti passes

Sutra – thread, string, line; condensed statements strung together to give an outline of a philosophy

Swadhisthana chakra – literally 'one's own abode'; psychic/pranic centre situated at the base of the spinal column, associated with the sacral plexus

Swami –'master of the self'; title of poorna sannyasins

Tantra – ancient universal science, philosophy and culture which deals with the transcendence of human nature from the present mundane level of evolution and understanding to the highest attainment of transcendental awareness, knowledge and experience; process of expansion of mind and liberation of energy; one of the six classical Indian philosophies

Tantric – pertaining to tantra

Tara – a goddess; a star

Tattwa – 'that-ness'; an element; primary substance; essence; truth; reality; principle

Tattwa nyasa – a tantric practice in which the essence of the basic elements is invoked and placed in different parts of the body

Trataka – to gaze steadily; a concentration practice

Udana – one of the pancha pranas located in the extremities of the arms, legs and head

Ugra – fierce, violent, ferocious, savage, cruel, fearful, powerful, strong, intense, sharp, hot

Ujjayi pranayama – often referred to as 'psychic breathing' as it is so successful in internalizing awareness and inducing meditative states. Performed by focusing the breath in the throat, contracting the epiglottis and producing a light snoring sound

Upanishad – 'to sit close by and listen'; ancient vedic texts, conveyed by sages, rishis or seers containing their experiences and teachings on the ultimate reality

Vedas – most ancient scriptural texts of India, composed before 5,000 BC, revealed to the sages and expressing knowledge of the whole universe; the four Vedas are: Rig, Yajur, Sama and Atharva

Vibhooti – sacred ash; psychic glory and power

Vidhi – doing, performance, practice, an act or action, method, manner, way, means, mode, sacred precept or rule, ordinance, injunction law, sacred command, rite

Vidya – higher knowledge, spiritual knowledge, science, lore, learning

Vijnanamaya kosha – astral or psychic (higher mental) sheath or body

Vishnu granthi – literally 'Vishnu's knot'; psychic knot in manipura and anahata chakras symbolizing the bondage of personal and emotional attachment

Vishuddhi chakra – psychic/pranic centre located at the level of the throat-pit or the thyroid gland; associated with the cervical plexus and particularly connected with purification and communication

Vyana – one of the pancha pranas pervading the whole body; reserve pranic energy

Yama – first limb of Patanjali's ashtanga yoga, the five self-restraints or rules of conduct pertaining to ethical perfection: *ahimsa,* non-violence; *satya,* truth; *asteya,* non-stealing; *brahmacharya,* continence and *aparigraha* non-covetousness

Yantra – geometric symbol designed for concentration or meditation in order to unleash the hidden potential within the consciousness; visual form of mantra used for concentration and meditation

Yashaswini – one of the seven minor nadis, flowing from the right big toe to the left ear

Yoga Vasishtha – monumental work on Vedanta in the form of a dialogue between Sri Rama and his guru, Sage Vasishtha

Yogi – an adept in yoga; one connected or endowed with yoga

Index of Practices

Chapter 13. Expansion, Relaxation and Contraction of Prana

Chapter 14. Distribution of Prana

Chapter 15. Self-Healing

Chapter 16. Healing Others

Chapter 17. Advanced Prana Vidya with the Masters

Notes

Notes

Notes